Report to the Committee on Energy and Commerce, House of Representatives

March 2013

NATIONAL PREPAREDNESS

Improvements Needed for Measuring Awardee Performance in Meeting Medical and Public Health Preparedness Goals

GAO

Accountability * Integrity * Reliability

GAO
Accountability * Integrity * Reliability

Highlights

Highlights of GAO-13-278, a report to the
Committee on Energy and Commerce, House
of Representatives

March 2013

NATIONAL PREPAREDNESS

Improvements Needed for Measuring Awardee Performance in Meeting Medical and Public Health Preparedness Goals

Why GAO Did This Study

HHS provides funding to the 50 states and 12 municipalities, territories, and freely associated states, primarily through ASPR's HPP and CDC's PHEP cooperative agreements, to help them build their capability to respond to emergencies such as hurricanes, pandemics, or terrorist events. The 62 awardees are to use this funding to help achieve the HPP goals of strengthening hospital preparedness and medical surge capacity and the PHEP goal of strengthening public health preparedness, and they must meet certain application, financial, and reporting requirements. GAO was asked about the effects of federal support on state and local response capabilities. GAO (1) assessed awardee progress in meeting HPP goals and how ASPR measures that progress, (2) assessed awardee progress in meeting the PHEP goal and how CDC measures that progress, and (3) identified the mechanisms HHS uses to ensure that awardees are meeting application, financial, and reporting requirements. GAO reviewed HPP and PHEP guidance, performance measures, and other documents; interviewed HHS officials; and analyzed HPP and PHEP data for fiscal years 2007 through 2011.

What GAO Recommends

GAO recommends that (1) HHS develop objective and quantifiable performance targets and incremental milestones tied to HPP and PHEP performance measures and (2) ensure that measures remain consistent and comparable to sufficiently measure progress. HHS generally agreed with GAO's recommendations but indicated that it would not be able to fully implement them for several years.

View GAO-13-278. For more information, contact Marcia Crosse at (202) 512-7114 or crossem@gao.gov.

What GAO Found

Available measures and awardee data provide some evidence that Hospital Preparedness Program (HPP) awardees have generally made progress in carrying out activities to achieve medical preparedness goals; however, the Department of Health and Human Services (HHS) Office of the Assistant Secretary for Preparedness and Response (ASPR) lacked a comprehensive performance management system to fully assess awardee progress. According to prior GAO work and the GPRA Modernization Act of 2010 (GPRAMA), successful performance measurement systems should include a select set of performance measures tied to realistically achievable targets with clearly defined milestones. GAO's analysis of ASPR data showed general progress. For example, the percentage of all 62 awardees' participating hospitals with medical evacuation and shelter-in-place plans increased from 79.9 percent to 88.3 percent from fiscal year 2007 to fiscal year 2011. However, while ASPR collected data on a range of activities, it did not have consistent performance measures and targets in place across this entire period. Beginning with fiscal year 2012, ASPR developed new provisional performance measures for the eight new capabilities that awardees are to use for HPP planning for the next 5 years and set 5-year targets for these measures. However, it did not develop annual milestones, which may make it difficult for ASPR and awardees to assess incremental progress toward meeting HPP goals.

Although Public Health Emergency Preparedness (PHEP) program awardees are improving in their ability to carry out preparedness activities, HHS's Centers for Disease Control and Prevention (CDC) lacked a consistent set of performance measures and targets to adequately assess the degree of awardee progress toward meeting the PHEP goal. For example, from fiscal years 2007 through 2011, the number of measures ranged from 5 to 30 in any one year, and CDC had only four targets for any of them. GAO's analysis of CDC data showed general progress on the measures. For example, for one measure, the average time it took the 62 awardees to assemble appropriate response staff decreased from 35 minutes in 2007 to 31 minutes in 2011, although the 50 state awardees did not always meet the 60-minute target that CDC set for them starting in 2009. Beginning with fiscal year 2012, CDC released 47 provisional performance measures for 14 of the 15 new PHEP capabilities but developed only four associated targets. Without consistent performance measures and associated targets, in accordance with prior GAO work and GPRAMA, CDC may not be able to assess how awardees are making progress toward meeting the PHEP goal.

HHS uses internal databases, site visits, and audit reports to help awardees meet HPP and PHEP application, financial, and reporting requirements. ASPR and CDC use internal databases to generate reports on awardee progress in meeting application renewal and reporting deadlines, to assess application completeness, and to periodically query databases in order to review financial information. They also conduct regular site visits and review state and federal audit reports to help awardees meet program requirements and assess awardees' use of funds. ASPR and CDC require awardees that have problems managing their HPP or PHEP funds to complete corrective action plans, and they restrict awardees' access to funds in more serious cases.

Contents

Tables

Figures

Abbreviations

ASPR	Office of the Assistant Secretary for Preparedness and Response
CDC	Centers for Disease Control and Prevention
CRI	Cities Readiness Initiative
ESAR-VHP	Emergency System for Advance Registration of Volunteer Health Professionals
GPRAMA	GPRA Modernization Act of 2010
HHS	Department of Health and Human Services
HPP	Hospital Preparedness Program
IOM	Institute of Medicine
NIMS	National Incident Management System
OIG	HHS Office of the Inspector General
OMB	Office of Management and Budget
PAHPA	Pandemic and All-Hazards Preparedness Act of 2006
PHEP	Public Health Emergency Preparedness program

March 22, 2013

The Honorable Fred Upton
Chairman
The Honorable Henry Waxman
Ranking Member
Committee on Energy and Commerce
House of Representatives

The 2011 and 2012 tornadoes in the Midwest, Hurricanes Sandy in 2012 and Katrina in 2005, the 2009 H1N1 influenza pandemic, and other emergencies have raised concerns about communities' and states' abilities to plan, prepare for, and respond to public health threats, whether naturally occurring or man-made. Of particular concern are questions about the ability of health care systems to "surge"—that is, to have the staff and resources in place to adequately care for increased numbers of affected individuals or individuals with unusual or highly specialized needs. Emergency preparedness experts agree that a natural disaster, infectious disease outbreak, or intentional terrorist attack that results in widespread injury or death could quickly overwhelm health care and public health systems, severely delaying the delivery of, or potentially compromising the quality of, critical medical services.[1] The Department of Health and Human Services (HHS) is the federal agency primarily responsible for assisting health care systems and state and local health departments in building their capacity and capability to prepare for and respond to public health emergencies, including mass casualty events.[2]

HHS provides funding for medical and public health preparedness primarily through two cooperative agreement programs—the Hospital Preparedness Program (HPP) and the Public Health Emergency

---

[1] Health care systems include hospitals and can also include emergency medical systems, long-term care facilities, and other health care entities.

[2] HHS also coordinates preparedness programs and activities at the federal level. These programs and activities include the National Disaster Medical System, a system of medical and public health personnel designed to augment state and local responders in public health emergencies, and the Public Health Emergency Medical Countermeasures Enterprise, an interagency group charged with providing strategic direction and priorities for developing and acquiring medical countermeasures—drugs, vaccines, and devices to diagnose, treat, prevent, or mitigate potential effects of exposure to chemical, biological, radiological, and nuclear agents and pandemic influenza.

Preparedness (PHEP) program.[3] From fiscal years 2002 through 2011, HHS awarded almost $12 billion to 62 entities, including the 50 states and 12 localities, U.S. territories, and freely associated states, to help them achieve the programs' medical and public health preparedness goals.[4] The goals of HPP—which is administered by HHS's Office of the Assistant Secretary for Preparedness and Response (ASPR)—are to improve medical surge capacity and enhance community and hospital preparedness for public health emergencies. The goal of PHEP—which is administered by HHS's Centers for Disease Control and Prevention (CDC)—is to strengthen state and local public health departments' ability to respond to a variety of public health emergencies. The 62 awardees are to use HPP and PHEP funding to carry out certain activities to achieve these goals, such as establishing electronic systems to track available hospital beds and other resources and building laboratory capabilities. To qualify for and receive cooperative agreement funding, awardees must also meet certain application, financial, and reporting requirements.

We and others have reported on the nation's ability to address the medical and public health consequences of emergencies. Since 2003, we have periodically reported on HPP and PHEP awardees' progress in achieving HPP and PHEP goals and HHS's management of HPP and PHEP awardee performance. We have found that awardees have made some improvements in preparedness but that additional guidance and

---

[3]A cooperative agreement is a legal instrument used to provide financial support when substantial interaction is expected between a federal agency and a state, local government, or other recipient carrying out the funded activity.

[4]The 62 entities comprise all 50 states, the District of Columbia, three large localities (Chicago, Los Angeles County, and New York City), and the eight U.S. territories and freely-associated states—American Samoa, the Commonwealths of the Northern Mariana Islands and Puerto Rico, the Federated States of Micronesia, Guam, the Republics of the Marshall Islands and Palau, and the U.S. Virgin Islands.

oversight were needed.[5] For example, in 2007 we reported concerns about the lack of standard analyses or reports that would enable HHS to compare data across HPP and PHEP awardees to measure collective progress, compare progress across awardees' programs, or provide consistent feedback to awardees, and we reported on the ongoing changes to HHS's performance management systems for these programs.[6] HHS and other organizations have reported that while progress has been made, the degree to which individual states, territories, and local jurisdictions are prepared to address large-scale health threats varies considerably and significant work remains to build medical and public health capabilities.[7] In addition, recent public health emergencies such as Hurricane Sandy have shown that while states have improved in their ability to effectively respond to a public health emergency as a result of receiving HPP and PHEP funds, their responses have also revealed gaps, for example, in planning for and carrying out hospital evacuations.

You asked us to examine the effects of federal funding for medical and public health preparedness on improving the readiness of health systems to manage public health emergencies, including mass casualty events. Our review (1) assesses the progress that awardees have made in meeting the medical preparedness goals of the HPP cooperative agreement program and how ASPR measures that progress, (2) assesses the progress that awardees have made in meeting the public health preparedness goal of the PHEP cooperative agreement

---

[5]See GAO, *Bioterrorism: Preparedness Varied across State and Local Jurisdictions,* GAO-03-373 (Washington, D.C.: Apr. 7, 2003); *Hospital Preparedness: Most Urban Hospitals Have Emergency Response Plans but Lack Certain Capacities for Bioterrorism Response,* GAO-03-924 (Washington, D.C.: Aug. 6, 2003); *HHS Bioterrorism Preparedness Programs: States Reported Progress but Fell Short of Program Goals for 2002,* GAO-04-360R (Washington, D.C.: Feb. 10, 2004); *Public Health and Hospital Emergency Preparedness: Evolution of Performance Measurement Systems to Measure Progress,* GAO-07-485R (Washington, D.C.: Mar. 23, 2007); and *Emergency Preparedness: States Are Planning for Medical Surge but Could Benefit from Shared Guidance for Allocating Scarce Medical Resources,* GAO-08-668 (Washington, D.C.: June 13, 2008).

[6]GAO-07-485R.

[7]See Department of Health and Human Services, *National Health Security Strategy* (Washington, D.C.: December 2009), and Trust for America's Health, *Ready or Not? Protecting the Public's Health from Diseases, Disasters, and Bioterrorism* (Washington, D.C.: December 2012).

program and how CDC measures that progress, and (3) identifies the mechanisms HHS uses to help ensure that state and local awardees are meeting the application, financial, and reporting requirements of the cooperative agreements. We also provide additional information about the need for medical surge preparedness for mass casualty events, in light of existing hospital emergency department crowding, in appendix I.

To assess the progress awardees have made in meeting the medical and public health preparedness goals of the HPP and PHEP cooperative agreement programs and how ASPR and CDC measure that progress, we reviewed relevant laws and directives that outline criteria for medical and public health preparedness and performance measurement. We reviewed ASPR's and CDC's HPP and PHEP funding opportunity announcements and any available performance measure guidance for fiscal years 2007 through 2011 to identify any HPP and PHEP performance measures that corresponded to the programs' goals and ASPR's and CDC's processes for assessing awardees' performance on these measures.[8] We analyzed HPP and PHEP awardee-submitted end-of-year performance data for fiscal years 2007 through 2011 to compare awardee performance against any ASPR- and CDC-designated performance measures to determine awardee progress.[9] We analyzed agency-designated performance measures and awardee-submitted performance data that reflected key activities that HPP and PHEP awardees conduct to achieve the goals of the cooperative agreements. ASPR and CDC also collected data related to their measures that provided them with supporting information on HPP and PHEP activities. For the purposes of our analysis, we calculated percentages from HPP and PHEP awardee data to enable comparisons over time. We received ASPR-validated HPP data and CDC-validated PHEP data for fiscal years 2007 through 2010 and unvalidated HPP and PHEP data for fiscal year

---

[8]Individual budget, or fiscal, years for HPP and PHEP run from July 1 through June 30, which typically coincide with the dates of state fiscal years. For the purposes of this report, we refer to individual cooperative agreement budget years as fiscal years.

[9]We selected these years for our study period because we had previously conducted evaluations of HPP and PHEP through fiscal year 2006.

2011.[10] We determined that the ASPR and CDC data for all 5 years were sufficiently reliable for our purposes based on ASPR's and CDC's data validation and cleaning processes. We also reviewed GAO and other federal criteria on performance assessment, such as GAO's criteria for key elements of performance measurement systems and the GPRA Modernization Act of 2010 (GPRAMA), and compared ASPR's and CDC's systems to these criteria.[11] We interviewed ASPR and CDC officials about HPP and PHEP performance measures, their processes for collecting and analyzing HPP and PHEP awardee performance data, and the results of their analyses. We also interviewed officials from relevant professional associations and other experts from the American Hospital Association, the Association of State and Territorial Health Officials, the Institute of Medicine, the National Association of County and City Health Officials, the RAND Corporation,[12] and the University of Pittsburgh Medical Center's Center for Biosecurity[13] to better understand HPP and PHEP awardees' progress in meeting the medical and public health preparedness goals of HHS's cooperative agreements.

To identify the mechanisms that HHS uses to help ensure that awardees are meeting the application, financial, and reporting requirements of the cooperative agreements, we reviewed relevant laws and directives, agency policies, and HPP and PHEP funding opportunity announcements for fiscal years 2007 through 2011 to identify the requirements of the

---

[10]ASPR and CDC validate awardee-submitted data to help ensure the accuracy of the information. ASPR and CDC had not yet completed their validation of the HPP and PHEP data, which were due to ASPR on September 30, 2012 and to CDC on November 9, 2012, respectively, by the time we completed our analysis in December 2012. Based on discussions with ASPR and CDC officials about their data review and validation processes and our comparison of unvalidated data for fiscal year 2010 with validated data for the same year, we determined that the fiscal year 2011 unvalidated data were sufficiently reliable for our purposes.

[11]See GAO, *Managing for Results: Critical Actions for Measuring Performance*, GAO/T-GGD/AIMD-95-187 (Washington, D.C.: June 20, 1995), and Pub. L. No. 111-352, § 3, 124 Stat. 3866, 3867 (2011) (codified at 31 U.S.C. § 1115). GPRAMA amends the Government Performance and Results Act of 1993 (GPRA), Pub. L. No. 103-62, 107 Stat. 285 (1993).

[12]The RAND Corporation has developed tools to help awardees self-assess certain of their PHEP activities and has contracted with CDC to conduct evaluations of awardee activities for the agency.

[13]ASPR previously contracted with the Center for Biosecurity to conduct evaluations of HPP.

cooperative agreements. We reviewed ASPR's and CDC's policies and procedures for overseeing cooperative agreement programs, such as HHS's *Grants Policy Statement* and CDC's *Financial Reference Guide for Grantees*, and other policies and procedures for monitoring awardee compliance with requirements. We reviewed documentation of any actions ASPR and CDC had taken in fiscal years 2007 through 2011 against awardees for not meeting cooperative agreement requirements, including any instances in which HHS found awardees to be using funds inappropriately. We interviewed ASPR and CDC officials about HPP and PHEP program requirements, how they monitor awardees' efforts in meeting cooperative agreement requirements, and actions they take to resolve situations in which awardees are not meeting requirements.

We conducted this performance audit from May 2012 through March 2013 in accordance with generally accepted government auditing standards. Those standards require that we plan and perform the audit to obtain sufficient, appropriate evidence to provide a reasonable basis for our findings and conclusions based on our audit objectives. We believe that the evidence obtained provides a reasonable basis for our findings and conclusions based on our audit objectives.

Background

The HPP and PHEP programs were established under the Public Health Security and Bioterrorism Preparedness and Response Act of 2002[14] and reauthorized under the Pandemic and All-Hazards Preparedness Act (PAHPA) in 2006.[15] HHS provides HPP and PHEP cooperative agreement funds[16] annually to the 50 states and 12 localities, territories,

---

[14]Pub. L. No. 107-188, §§ 131,116 Stat. 594, 617 (codified as amended at 42 U.S.C. §§ 247d-3a, 3b).

[15]PAHPA transferred oversight of HPP from HHS's Health Resources and Services Administration to ASPR, which was also established under this law, and shifted HPP from a bioterrorism-specific to an all-hazards focus, which includes naturally occurring disasters, disease outbreaks, and man-made events such as terrorist attacks. Pub. L. No. 109-417, §§ 101, 102, 201, 120 Stat. 2831, 2832, 2837 (2006) (codified at 42 U.S.C. §§ 247d-3a, 3b and 42 U.S.C. § 300hh-10).

[16]HHS has also made other funds available in past years for state and local medical and public health preparedness for pandemic influenza, health care facility partnerships, and public health emergency response to specific public health events, such as 2009's H1N1 influenza pandemic.

and freely associated states.[17] These 62 awardees are to use the funds to carry out certain preparedness activities to achieve the goals of the programs and are to fulfill certain application, financial, and reporting requirements of the cooperative agreements.[18]

HPP Activities to Achieve Medical Preparedness Goals

To achieve the HPP medical preparedness goals of improving medical surge capacity and enhancing hospital preparedness, awardees are to use HPP funds to conduct certain activities and accumulate certain resources:[19]

- establishing and maintaining electronic systems to track available hospital beds and other resources through the National Hospital Available Beds for Emergencies and Disasters system;

- establishing and maintaining Emergency System for Advance Registration of Volunteer Health Professionals (ESAR-VHP) networks—which consist of electronic systems to register, track, and verify the credentials of volunteer health care providers to assist with medical surge during public health emergencies;

- developing health care coalitions and partnerships—networks of health care facilities that can provide medical services, resources, or support during a public health emergency;[20]

- educating and training health care workers;

---

[17]HPP and PHEP funds are distributed to the 62 awardees using a formula that includes a base amount for each awardee plus population-based funding.

[18]The 62 awardees in turn provide subawards, which generally go to hospitals or other health care facilities for HPP and local and tribal public health departments for PHEP, to assist in carrying out HPP and PHEP activities at the local level.

[19]These activities were outlined in ASPR's HPP funding opportunity announcements for fiscal years 2007 through 2011.

[20]For fiscal year 2012, ASPR shifted the focus of HPP from individual hospitals and health care facilities to health care coalitions, with awardees expected to develop or refine existing coalitions over a multiyear project cycle, and collected data at the coalition level rather than the hospital level.

GAO-13-278 Medical and Public Health Preparedness

- implementing and maintaining National Incident Management System (NIMS) activities;[21]

- engaging with other responders through interoperable communications systems;

- establishing, maintaining, or enhancing medical countermeasure caches to protect health care workers during an emergency;

- enhancing mass fatality management and evacuation and shelter-in-place plans; and

- exercising and improving awardee preparedness plans and coordinating regional exercises.

HPP awardees are to prioritize these activities based on the medical preparedness needs of their jurisdictions.[22] ASPR provides technical assistance to support awardees in planning or carrying out program activities and conducts routine site visits to assess awardee activities, progress, and challenges. ASPR collects midyear and end-of-year performance data from awardees on how they are carrying out program activities and accumulating resources.

PHEP Activities to Achieve Public Health Preparedness Goal

To achieve the PHEP public health preparedness goal of strengthening the ability of public health departments to respond to public health emergencies, awardees are to use PHEP funds to conduct certain activities:[23]

---

[21]NIMS is a federally adopted standardized approach to all-hazards incident management that is designed to be flexible and scalable based on the characteristics of a particular event. HPP implementation and maintenance activities for NIMS include adopting NIMS throughout health care systems; incorporating NIMS principles into planning; identifying and training appropriate personnel in NIMS concepts and principles; ensuring interoperability of communications systems; and managing all emergencies and events, including information for the public, in accordance with NIMS and the incident command system for managing resources during an emergency.

[22]To determine needs and prioritize activities, awardees are to identify hazards that their jurisdictions may be likely to face and any associated health care vulnerabilities and rank the risk of each hazard to the jurisdictions.

[23]These activities were outlined in CDC's PHEP funding opportunity announcements for fiscal years 2007 through 2011.

- developing plans to receive, store, distribute, and dispense medical countermeasures during a public health emergency;[24]

- testing awardees' ability to notify and assemble appropriate response staff during an emergency;

- building laboratory capability for testing and identifying harmful pathogens and reporting results to CDC;[25]

- communicating health, risk, and other information in a timely manner to the public in public health emergencies;

- conducting drills and exercises to test the above response capabilities and activities; and

- completing after-action reports and improvement plans to improve response times and activities for future drills, exercises, or real events.

PHEP awardees are to prioritize these activities based on their jurisdictional public health preparedness needs. CDC provides technical assistance to support PHEP awardees in planning or carrying out program activities and conducts routine site visits to assess awardee activities, progress, and challenges. CDC collects end-of-year performance data from awardees on how they are carrying out program activities.

---

[24]Under PHEP, CDC also provides additional funding to 72 metropolitan statistical areas for their countermeasure dispensing activities, under a program known as the Cities Readiness Initiative (CRI). The Office of Management and Budget (OMB) defines a metropolitan statistical area as a region with at least one urbanized area that has a population of at least 50,000 and comprises the central county or counties containing the core, plus adjacent outlying counties having a high degree of social and economic integration with the central county or counties as measured through commuting.

[25]Under PHEP, CDC also provides additional funding to 10 chemical laboratories—which the agency designates as level 1 laboratories—that serve as surge capacity laboratories for CDC. The 10 level 1 chemical laboratory awardees must use this funding to address chemical emergency response surge capacity needs, including maintaining adequate numbers of staff and laboratory equipment; maintaining the ability to conduct testing and quality assurance in case of a public health emergency; training and proficiency testing for laboratory staff; and participating in local, state, and national exercises.

HPP and PHEP Application, Financial, and Reporting Requirements

Applicants and awardees are to fulfill certain application, financial, and reporting requirements as part of the terms of the HPP and PHEP cooperative agreements. To continue to receive HPP and PHEP funding, awardees must reapply annually. Applications are typically due 60 calendar days after the funding opportunity announcement is posted on the federal grants website. When they reapply for HPP or PHEP funding, awardees are required to submit detailed budget information and plans for how they will use the funds in the fiscal year to carry out preparedness activities.[26] For fiscal year 2012, ASPR and CDC have aligned the HPP and PHEP programs in several ways. For example, ASPR and CDC set a 5-year project cycle for both programs and aligned the individual HPP and PHEP fiscal years within the 5-year cycle.[27] In March 2012, ASPR and CDC issued a joint funding opportunity announcement for HPP and PHEP. Awardees were required to submit a single application to reapply for both programs, and HPP and PHEP awards were issued together.

Awardees must also meet certain financial and audit requirements and submit periodic reports. Financial requirements include providing matching nonfederal funds in the amount of 10 percent of HPP and PHEP annual awards, maintaining state funding, and adhering to ASPR and CDC guidelines for the appropriate use of cooperative agreement funds.[28] Audit requirements include undergoing biennial financial audits of their cooperative agreement funds as required by PAHPA. ASPR and CDC

---

[26]HPP and PHEP awardees are asked to include in these plans descriptions of how they will coordinate health care and public health preparedness activities across the two programs and integrate preparedness activities with other governmental and nongovernmental partners, such as homeland security and emergency management agencies and emergency medical services organizations, as well as citizen representative groups, to better leverage community resources.

[27]The HPP and PHEP 5-year project cycle began July 1, 2012. Under the new 5-year cycle, awardees are still required to reapply annually for funding and provide annual budgets and updated work plans for HHS approval.

[28]The match requirement does not apply to the three localities of Chicago, New York, and Los Angeles County. In addition, pursuant to HHS's grants policy, match requirements, including in-kind donations, of less than $200,000 are waived with respect to cooperative agreements to the governments of American Samoa, Guam, the Northern Mariana Islands, and the Virgin Islands. Awardees must also demonstrate that they can maintain state expenditures for HPP and PHEP activities at a level no less than the average of their expenditures for the preceding 2-year period. Restrictions on the use of cooperative agreement funds are laid out in the funding opportunity announcements and include prohibitions on the use of funds for such activities as research, lobbying, and clinical care.

expect awardees to comply with Office of Management and Budget (OMB) A-133 audit requirements for those awardees that expend $500,000 or more in total federal funds per year.[29] ASPR and CDC consider awardees that satisfy OMB audit requirements as satisfying PAHPA's biennial audit requirement provided they include HPP and PHEP expenditures in their A-133 audits. Awardees are also required to submit midyear and end-of-year progress reports and periodic financial reports. ASPR and CDC specify the time frames for these reports in the HPP and PHEP funding opportunity announcements. ASPR and CDC conduct site visits and provide technical assistance to support HPP and PHEP awardees in meeting application, financial, and reporting requirements.

PAHPA directed HHS to develop and implement by 2009 measurable, evidence-based benchmarks to assess the level of awardee preparedness. Beginning with fiscal year 2009, awardees were required to meet all benchmarks subject to withholding of funds, as stipulated by PAHPA. HHS is to give entities that fail to substantively meet these benchmarks the opportunity to correct their noncompliance and is to withhold funds from those entities that fail to correct noncompliance.[30] ASPR and CDC have designated as benchmarks some of the HPP- and PHEP-funded activities, such as HPP awardees' ability to generate a list of potential volunteer health professionals available to assist in a public health emergency and PHEP awardees' ability to receive, store, and dispense medical countermeasures. Other benchmarks subject to withholding reflect HPP and PHEP program requirements, such as adhering to all reporting deadlines.

Performance Measurement

Performance measurement is the ongoing monitoring and reporting of program accomplishments, particularly progress toward preestablished

---

[29]The Single Audit Act, as amended, requires all nonfederal entities (states, local governments, and nonprofit organizations) that expend $500,000 or more in federal awards per year to obtain an annual audit in accordance with specified criteria. See 31 U.S.C. §§ 7501 et seq. Accordingly, OMB issued Circular A-133, *Audits of States, Local Governments, and Non-Profit Organizations*, setting forth standards for obtaining consistency and uniformity among federal agencies for the audit of states, local governments, and nonprofit organizations expending federal awards.

[30]Pub. L. No. 109-417, § 201, 120 Stat. 2837 (pertinent provision codified at 42 U.S.C. § 247d-3a(g)).

goals, and focuses on whether a program has achieved its objectives, expressed as measurable performance standards. Performance measures may address the type or level of program activities conducted (process), the direct products and services delivered by a program (outputs), or the results of those products and services (outcomes).[31] Performance measurement systems should include not only the collection of data on various metrics, but also a designation of specific performance measures, with realistically achievable performance targets against which to measure progress.[32] Successful performance measurement systems typically produce measures that are outcome-linked, significant, responsive to multiple priorities, and based on credible information. According to GPRAMA, performance measures for federal programs must provide a basis for comparing actual program results with established performance targets—which should be objective, quantifiable, and measureable—and clearly defined milestones.[33]

HPP Awardees Have Generally Made Progress in Carrying Out Medical Preparedness Activities and Accumulating Resources, but ASPR Cannot Thoroughly Assess Their Performance

Available data show that HPP awardees have generally made progress in their ability to conduct medical preparedness activities and accumulate resources required under the cooperative agreement from fiscal years 2007 through 2011. However, ASPR lacked a comprehensive performance management system during this period, so we could only identify some trends in performance over time, using awardee data from end-of-year reports. Although ASPR has made efforts to develop a more comprehensive performance management system for the new project cycle beginning in fiscal year 2012, it may not have realistic performance targets and milestones needed to assess awardee progress in meeting short- and long-term HPP preparedness goals.

---

[31]GAO, *Performance Measurement and Evaluation: Definitions and Relationships*, GAO-11-646SP (Washington, D.C.: May 2011).

[32]GAO/T-GGD/AIMD-95-187.

[33]Pub. L. No. 111-352, § 3, 124 Stat. 3867 (pertinent provision codified at 31 U.S.C. § 1115(b)).

An Increasing Number of HPP Awardees Have Been Carrying Out Medical Preparedness Activities and Accumulating Resources

In fiscal years 2007 through 2011, ASPR collected performance data from awardees on how they were carrying out HPP activities and organized the data into what ASPR designated as 14 elements of medical preparedness; ASPR also specified performance measures and targets for some of the data collected under the preparedness elements in certain years. For 11 of the 14 elements, ASPR collected data that describe the number of awardees or their participating hospitals that have executed, or have the capability of executing, particular activities or tasks, such as adopting NIMS, conducting preparedness exercises, developing specific plans for managing mass fatalities and medical evacuations, and reporting bed availability on request within a given amount of time. For the remaining 3 elements, ASPR collected data that provided it with more information on its awardees' resources—such as the number of available medical countermeasures and the number of telecommunications service priority lines funded by HPP.[34] Every year, awardees must report on their ability, and the ability of their participating hospitals, to conduct the activities and accumulate the resources under the HPP preparedness elements. Table 1 shows 12 of the 14 preparedness elements, along with 17 activities and resources—which we refer to as metrics—for which data were collected from fiscal years 2007 through 2011.[35] Data collected for the remaining 2 preparedness elements—"medical countermeasures" and "telecommunications service priority"—reflect a single count at a specific point in time and therefore could not be evaluated across our study period. ASPR also designated some performance measures in fiscal years 2007 and 2008 for the data it collected under the 14 preparedness elements.[36] For example, in fiscal years 2007 and 2008, for the preparedness element "emergency medical volunteers," ASPR collected

---

[34]Telecommunications Service Priority is a program that authorizes national security and emergency preparedness organizations to receive priority treatment for vital voice and data circuits or other telecommunications services. It provides service vendors with a Federal Communications Commission mandate to prioritize requests by identifying those services critical to national security and emergency preparedness.

[35]We analyzed the metrics that reflected the key activities for each preparedness element across all 5 years of our study period. ASPR also collected data that provided additional information about these activities. For example, for the preparedness element "hospital bed availability," ASPR also collected data on numbers of eight different bed types—including medical/surgical beds, burn beds, and pediatric beds—available at a given point in time.

[36]Because ASPR had specified performance measures for the first 2 years of our study period only, we could not evaluate awardee performance against these measures during the entire study period.

data for a performance measure on each individual awardee's ability to generate a list of potential volunteer health professionals within 2 hours of an HHS request, and for the preparedness element "hospital bed availability," ASPR collected data for a performance measure on the number of awardees' participating hospitals that could report available beds to the state emergency operations center within 60 minutes of the state's request. During these 2 years, ASPR specified a total of 13 performance measures for the data collected under the preparedness elements, with the number of measures varying in each year. In fiscal year 2007, ASPR collected data for 6 clearly defined performance measures with corresponding targets; for fiscal year 2008, ASPR kept 5 of these measures and added 7 new ones. (See app. II for the fiscal years 2007 and 2008 performance measures.) Although ASPR did not designate any performance measures for the data collected under the preparedness elements for fiscal years 2009 through 2011 in its guidance to awardees, it continued to collect much of the same information as collected in previous years with some modifications as reflected in the metrics we analyzed.[37] For example, for fiscal years 2009 through 2011, ASPR continued to collect data on the number of hospitals that demonstrated dedicated, redundant communications during an exercise or event, which it designated as a performance measure in fiscal years 2007 and 2008.

---

[37]As authorized by PAHPA, ASPR converted three of the 2008 performance measures into benchmarks subject to withholding for fiscal years 2009 through 2011. Officials told us they selected as benchmarks subject to withholding those areas they considered to be essential to the execution of HPP, such as timely reporting and the ability to exercise a plan. ASPR continued to collect data on awardee activities related to the other measures as part of its data collection efforts but did not specify performance measures for these activities.

Table 1: Hospital Preparedness Program (HPP) Metrics for 12 of the 14 Preparedness Elements, Fiscal Years 2007 through 2011

Communications systems
- Number of participating hospitals that demonstrated dedicated, redundant communications during an exercise or event

Decontamination
- Number of ambulatory and nonambulatory patients that can be decontaminated by awardee within a 3-hour period

Education and training
- Number of participating hospitals that have identified appropriate personnel for training
- Number of participating hospitals that have verified completion of training by appropriate personnel

Emergency medical volunteers
- Number of awardees that can generate a verified list of available volunteers registered in an Emergency System for Advance Registration of Volunteer Health Professionals (ESAR-VHP) system within 24 hours of a request being issued by a requesting body or HHS Secretary's Operations Center
- Total ESAR-VHP volunteers registered by awardees

Fatality management plans
- Number of participating hospitals with mass fatality management plans

Hospital bed availability
- Number of participating hospitals that are able to report bed availability to the state emergency operations center within 60 minutes of a request
- Number of awardees that are able to report bed availability to the HHS Secretary's Operations Center or other federal partner within 4 hours of a request

Isolation
- Number of awardee regions that can maintain patients in negative pressure isolation in emergency departments
- Number of awardee regions that can maintain patients in negative pressure isolation in nonemergency-department settings

Laboratory referral
- Number of awardee's laboratory personnel trained in protocols for clinical sample referral to public health laboratories

Medical evacuation and shelter-in-place plans
- Number of participating hospitals with evacuation and shelter-in-place plans

National Incident Management System (NIMS)
- Number of participating hospitals that have adopted NIMS

Partnerships
- Number of awardees with memorandums of understanding reported

Preparedness exercises
- Number of participating hospitals that took part in an exercise or event
- Number of participating hospitals that developed written improvement plans based on after-action reports

Source: GAO summary of ASPR preparedness elements and selected metrics.

Notes: Data collected for the remaining 2 preparedness elements—"medical countermeasures" and "telecommunications service priority"—reflect a single count at a specific point in time and therefore could not be evaluated across our study period. We analyzed the metrics that reflected the key activities for each preparedness element. ASPR also collected data that provide additional information about these activities. For example, for the preparedness element "hospital bed availability," ASPR also collected data on numbers of eight different bed types—including medical/surgical beds, burn beds, and pediatric beds—available at a given point in time.

In fiscal year 2007, ASPR collected much of the same data it collected in subsequent years, but data collection was not formally organized by preparedness element.

From fiscal year 2007 through fiscal year 2011, an increasing number of the 62 HPP awardees and their participating hospitals showed progress or performed steadily in 15 of the 17 metrics we reviewed, despite some variation in year-to-year performance.[38] (See app. III for the results of our analysis for each of the 17 metrics.) For example, for the "medical evacuation planning" preparedness element the percentage of all awardees' participating hospitals with medical evacuation and shelter-in-place plans increased from 79.9 percent to 88.3 percent from fiscal year 2007 to fiscal year 2011. However, while the average percentage of participating hospitals with these plans increased over this period, there was wide variation among awardees in fiscal year 2011 in the percentage of their participating hospitals that had plans. For example, for 23 of the 62 awardees, 100 percent of their participating hospitals had medical evacuation and shelter-in-place plans in 2011. Conversely, for 22 awardees the percentage of participating hospitals with medical evacuation and shelter-in-place plans was below the average of 88.3 percent, and for 3 of these the percentage fell below 50 percent.

Similarly, there was also an increase associated with the "partnerships" preparedness element. ASPR measures awardees' efforts in building health care coalitions or partnerships by collecting data on memorandums of understanding between participating hospitals, which it has done only since fiscal year 2008. In fiscal year 2011, 61 of the 62 awardees reported that hospitals within their areas had memorandums of understanding between participating hospitals to facilitate care in the event of a disaster.[39]

In another example, for the preparedness element "emergency medical volunteers," the number of volunteer health professionals that awardees registered through ESAR-VHP systems increased 34 percent from fiscal year 2007 through fiscal year 2011, with an average of almost 3,200 volunteers registered per awardee in fiscal year 2011. However, individual awardees varied widely in fiscal year 2011 in terms of the

---

[38]In fiscal year 2007, ASPR collected much of the same activity and resource data it collected in subsequent years, but data collection was not formally organized by preparedness element.

[39]The 61 awardees reported 593 health care coalitions in fiscal year 2011.

number of volunteers registered, from 119 for one awardee to 20,415 for another, which may be due in part to differences in awardee population size.[40] In addition, more awardees were able to use their ESAR-VHP systems to generate a verified list of available volunteer professionals.[41] In fiscal year 2011, 61 of the 62 awardees were able to submit a verified list of available volunteer professionals within 24 hours of a request being received, which was about a 10 percent increase from fiscal year 2007. In fiscal years 2007 and 2008, ASPR's performance measure for this activity specified a target time of 2 hours for awardees to generate a list of potential volunteers. In fiscal year 2007, 55 awardees were able to generate the list within the target time, and in fiscal year 2008, 58 awardees were able to do so.

The 2 metrics in which awardees' participating hospitals did not make progress were in the "hospital bed availability" and "preparedness exercises" preparedness elements. For example, for hospital bed availability, HPP required that participating hospitals be tested on their ability to report available beds to the state emergency operations center within 60 minutes of a request, which ASPR designated as a performance measure in fiscal years 2007 and 2008. The overall number of participating HPP hospitals able to carry out this activity increased slightly from 4,713 to 4,823 from fiscal year 2007 through fiscal year 2010.[42] However, in fiscal year 2011, the number of participating hospitals able to report available beds within 60 minutes declined to 4,688, which is below the fiscal year 2007 number. Additionally, the percentage of all HPP hospitals able to report within 60 minutes declined from 91.7 percent in fiscal year 2007 to 87.6 percent in fiscal year 2011. In fiscal year 2011, 36 awardees reported that 100 percent of their participating hospitals could report available beds within the required time frame, while 4 awardees reported that less than 50 percent of their participating hospitals could report bed availability within 60 minutes. Awardees have been relatively consistent in their ability to report available beds since fiscal year 2008,

---

[40]The range of registered volunteers excludes data from the eight U.S. territories and freely associated states.

[41]ASPR requires awardees to submit information on the number of registered volunteer health professionals by health profession, such as physicians, registered nurses, and pharmacists, as well as by credential level.

[42]Awardees report beds by type—burn beds or pediatric beds, for example—and indicate whether they are staffed or available within 24 hours in the event of an emergency.

when 37 awardees met the target of 100 percent of their participating hospitals reporting within 60 minutes. In fiscal year 2007, ASPR specified a target of 75 percent of an awardee's participating hospitals able to report within 60 minutes, and 56 awardees met this target for that fiscal year.

ASPR Has Not Been Able to Thoroughly Assess Awardee Performance with Its Existing Performance System

During fiscal years 2007 through 2011, ASPR lacked a comprehensive performance management system with clearly defined and consistent performance measures, corresponding targets, and milestones that would have provided it with a clear basis for assessing awardee accomplishments. According to our prior work, successful performance measurement systems include a designation of specific performance measures, with realistically achievable performance targets against which to measure progress.[43] Additionally, as outlined in GPRAMA, performance targets should be objective, quantifiable, and measureable, with clearly defined milestones.[44] We previously examined HHS's performance measurement system for HPP and found that HHS had been collecting data on HPP awardee performance since 2002, even as the system was modified several times from 2002 through 2006.[45] According to officials, when HPP was transferred from HHS's Health Resources and Services Administration to ASPR in fiscal year 2007, ASPR maintained some of the existing performance measures where feasible and appropriate to help ensure program continuity and to identify trends in awardee activities.[46] ASPR also set corresponding targets for the performance measures in fiscal years 2007 and 2008. However, ASPR made modifications to the performance measures, targets, and awardee data between the time HPP was transferred to ASPR and fiscal year 2009, and officials told us that the type of data ASPR collected underwent notable changes during this time. While ASPR continued to collect performance data, beginning in fiscal year 2009 ASPR no longer designated specific performance measures or corresponding targets in its

---

[43]GAO/T-GGD/AIMD-95-187.

[44]Pub. L. No. 111-352, § 3, 124 Stat. 3867 (2011) (pertinent provision codified at 31 U.S.C. § 1115(b)).

[45]GAO-07-485R.

[46]Prior to March 2007, HPP was administered by HHS's Health Resources and Services Administration and was named the National Bioterrorism Hospital Preparedness Program.

HPP guidance.[47] ASPR officials stated that they consider all of the data they collected to be performance measures, with desired performance targets of 100 percent of awardees or their participating hospitals able to carry out the activities or accumulate the resources required. Our prior work on performance measurement has shown that performance measures should be limited to a vital few that provide the most needed information for accountability and program management.[48] Without a performance management system with clearly defined and consistent measures, targets, and milestones, ASPR could use the data it collected from awardees throughout the 5-year study period only to evaluate trends and obtain information and situational awareness about the program and awardees' and hospitals' preparedness activities.

According to ASPR officials, project officers use awardees' data as a tool to gauge the awardees' progress in carrying out HPP activities and accumulating the HPP resources. The project officers begin reviewing the data when the data are submitted, using the data to assess awardees' strengths, weaknesses, and areas of concern. ASPR officials also stated that if an awardee is not showing clear progress, they work with the awardee to determine what technical assistance—such as sharing best practices for tracking and reporting data or providing other support to help awardees address preparedness gaps—is needed to help the awardee improve. ASPR officials told us that in their opinion, data show that progress is being made toward having 100 percent of awardees and their participating hospitals carry out the HPP activities and accumulate the HPP resources.

In 2012, ASPR announced eight new health care preparedness capabilities, which provide a new organizing framework for HPP awardees' medical preparedness activities for fiscal year 2012 and beyond.[49] ASPR developed provisional performance measures, as well

---

[47]According to officials, during a fiscal year 2009 conference, ASPR told awardees that the expected target was that 100 percent of awardee hospitals would be able to carry out HPP activities.

[48]GAO/T-GGD/AIMD-95-187.

[49]Office of the Assistant Secretary for Preparedness and Response, *Healthcare Preparedness Capabilities: National Guidance for Healthcare System Preparedness* (Washington, D.C.: January 2012). The eight health care capabilities are emergency operations coordination, fatality management, health care system preparedness, health care system recovery, information sharing, medical surge, responder safety and health, and volunteer management.

as long-term performance targets for the measures, for each of these eight capabilities;[50] however, the associated performance targets may not be realistic in all cases. ASPR set the performance targets for these measures at 100 percent of awardees and health care coalitions achieving each measure by the end of the 5-year project cycle.[51] ASPR officials acknowledged that not all awardees may be able to achieve 100 percent of all eight capabilities because of budget constraints. Furthermore, ASPR officials indicated that they have not yet decided whether they would set short-term, interim performance milestones for awardees to help them gauge their progress in meeting the 5-year performance targets of 100 percent. ASPR officials stated that in order to develop any interim milestones, they would need to collect additional data for the new performance measures. Our previous work has emphasized the importance of ensuring that performance goals are realistically achievable.[52] In setting performance targets at 100 percent without milestones to help HHS and awardees gauge incremental progress throughout the 5-year cycle, ASPR has created a system that may not be realistically achievable.

---

[50]ASPR considers the new performance measures to be provisional, as they are subject to change based on initial awardee data. For fiscal year 2012, ASPR is requiring awardees to report on the measures during the midyear (January 31, 2013) and end-of-year (September 30, 2013) reporting cycles.

[51]Beginning in fiscal year 2012, ASPR has shifted the unit of measurement from awardees and their participating hospitals to awardees and their participating health care coalitions, which ASPR considers a collaborative network of health care organizations and their respective public- and private-sector response partners within a defined region.

[52]GAO/T-GGD/AIMD-95-187.

PHEP Awardees' Ability to Carry Out Some Public Health Preparedness Activities Has Improved, but CDC Lacks Performance Targets to Assess Overall Progress toward Goals

For fiscal years 2007 through 2011, PHEP awardees have made some progress in their ability to conduct preparedness activities to meet the program's public health preparedness goal. However, CDC lacked a comprehensive performance management system, including measures and targets that remained consistent over time. Therefore, we could only identify some trends in performance over time, using awardee data from end-of-year reports. Beginning in fiscal year 2012, CDC began a new 5-year project cycle and released 47 performance measures to assess awardee progress toward meeting the public health goal, but only 4 of these measures have associated performance targets. Without additional targets, CDC may not be able to fully assess awardee progress.

PHEP Awardees' Ability to Carry Out Some Preparedness Activities to Meet Goal Has Generally Improved, but Performance on Other Activities Has Remained Level or Declined

From fiscal year 2007 through fiscal year 2011, CDC collected performance data on how awardees carried out public health preparedness activities tied to specific agency-designated performance measures to meet the PHEP goal. CDC collected data on the time it took awardees to carry out certain activities, such as the time it took awardees to notify appropriate response staff and the time it took to develop messages for the public during a public health emergency.[53] CDC also collected other data under the performance measures, such as information on the type of activity for which staff members were notified or messages developed. During the study period, CDC collected information on a total of 32 agency-designated performance measures. The number of performance measures for which CDC collected information on awardee activities ranged from 5 to 30 in any one year of this period.[54] (See table 2 for the PHEP performance measures and corresponding targets for fiscal years 2007 through 2011.)

---

[53]CDC collects data for both real events and exercises in which awardees participate in a given fiscal year, and awardees can submit data for multiple events and exercises each year.

[54]In 2007, CDC collected information on five performance measures. In 2008, CDC discarded one measure and added two new performance measures, and the agency collected information on a total of six measures from fiscal year 2008 through fiscal year 2010. In fiscal year 2011, CDC discarded another measure and added 25 new measures, collecting information on a total of 30 performance measures.

Table 2: Public Health Emergency Preparedness (PHEP) Program Performance Measures and Targets, Fiscal Year 2007 through Fiscal Year 2011

Performance measure	2007	2008	2009	2010	2011
Pulsed-field gel electrophoresis (PFGE): percentage of PFGE subtyping data results for *Escherichia* (*E.*) *coli* and *Listeria* submitted to the PulseNet national database[a] within 4 working days of receiving isolate at the PFGE laboratory[b] *Target: 90 percent of samples submitted within 4 working days*	✓+	✓+	✓+	✓+	✓+
Staff notification: time to notify preidentified staff with public health agency incident management functional responsibilities *Target: 60 minutes (2007 only)*	✓+	✓	✓	✓	
Staff assembly: time for staff with public health agency incident management functional responsibilities to report for duty *Target: 60 minutes (applies to 50 state awardees only)[c]*	✓+	✓	✓+	✓+	✓+
Crisis and emergency response communication public message dissemination: time to issue a risk communication message for dissemination to the public		✓	✓	✓	✓
Communication: percentage of key response partners that public health agencies can successfully contact without using the electric power grid or primary landline telephone service	✓				
Incident action plan: production of the approved plan before the start of the second operational period		✓	✓	✓	✓
After-action report and improvement plan: time to complete a draft of a report and improvement plan	✓	✓	✓	✓	✓
Medical countermeasure dispensing and medical materiel management and distribution: composite measure, composed of operational drill scores and production of other planning materials[d]					✓
Public health surveillance and epidemiological investigation: consists of six performance measures, including the proportion of reports of selected reportable diseases received by a public health agency within the jurisdiction-required time and the proportion of reports of selected reportable diseases for which an initial public health control measure was initiated within the appropriate time frame[e]					✓
Public health laboratory testing: consists of 14 performance measures, including the time for laboratories to acknowledge receipt of an urgent message and time for the first laboratorian to report for duty at the laboratory[e] *Target: time to complete a notification between CDC, on-call laboratorian, and on-call epidemiologist (and vice versa) – 45 minutes (target applies to two performance measures for biological and chemical laboratories)*					✓+[f]
Community preparedness: consists of four performance measures, including the number of key organizations that local health departments identified for participation in public health preparedness efforts and the proportion of key organizations that engaged in preparedness activities[e]					✓

Legend: ✓ = performance measures applicable. + = performance targets applicable.

Source: GAO analysis of CDC information.

[a]PulseNet is a national network of public health, food, and regulatory agency laboratories coordinated by CDC. The network consists of state and local health department laboratories and other federal agency laboratories.

[b]PFGE is a laboratory method that allows researchers to use molecular patterns to identify the strain of an individual *E. coli* or *Listeria* bacterium.

GAO-13-278 Medical and Public Health Preparedness

[c]Beginning in fiscal year 2009, CDC designated a 60-minute performance target for the staff assembly performance measure for the 50 state awardees only. CDC did not specify a performance target for the staff assembly performance measure that applied to the territories and freely associated states for fiscal years 2009 through 2011. In 2007, CDC set a target of 2.5 hours for the 50 state awardees. In fiscal year 2008, CDC did not specify a performance target for any awardees.

[d]In fiscal year 2011, CDC developed a performance measure specific to medical countermeasure dispensing. Prior to fiscal year 2011, CDC scored awardees' medical countermeasure distribution and dispensing activities but did not designate a specific performance measure for them. However, from fiscal years 2007 through 2011, CDC required all awardees to conduct these activities and designated them as one of the PHEP benchmarks subject to withholding of funds, as stipulated by PAHPA.

[e]CDC introduced these performance measures in fiscal year 2011. Because CDC collected data on these measures for only 1 year of our study period, we did not analyze them and, therefore, did not list the individual measures in the table. For more information on these measures, see Centers for Disease Control and Prevention, *Public Health Emergency Preparedness Cooperative Agreement Budget Period 11 Performance Measures Specification and Guidance.* (Atlanta, Ga.: October 2011).

[f]These measures were developed in conjunction with CDC's Laboratory Response Network, which is responsible for maintaining an integrated network of state and local public health, federal, military, and international laboratories.

Awardees made improvements in carrying out activities for three of CDC's PHEP performance measures—pulsed-field gel electrophoresis,[55] staff notification, and staff assembly—according to our analysis of awardee data. For the performance measure on pulsed-field gel electrophoresis, awardees showed improvement in their ability to both test samples of *Escherichia* (*E.*) *coli* and *Listeria* and report test results to CDC's PulseNet[56] within the agency's designated performance target of 4 working days, from fiscal year 2007 through fiscal year 2011. The average percentage of tested *E. coli* samples submitted to PulseNet within 4 working days increased from 86.2 percent in fiscal year 2007 to 95.0 percent for all awardees in fiscal year 2011, gradually surpassing CDC's target of 90 percent of samples submitted within 4 days.[57] Awardees' ability to test and report *Listeria* samples also improved, from an average of 82.6 percent of samples submitted to PulseNet within 4 working days to an average of 92.2 percent. (See fig. 1.) During the data collection process for these measures, CDC asked awardees to explain why they may not have met a designated performance target. In

---

[55]Pulsed-field gel electrophoresis is a laboratory method that allows researchers to use molecular patterns to identify the strain of an individual *E. coli* or *Listeria* bacterium.

[56]PulseNet is a national network of public health food and regulatory agency laboratories coordinated by CDC. The network consists of state and local health department laboratories and other federal agency laboratories.

[57]While the national average gradually reached CDC's 90 percent goal in 2011, some individual awardees met or exceeded this goal in prior years.

2010, for example, awardees cited issues such as staffing or funding shortages and technical problems with laboratory instruments that led to delays in reporting.

Figure 1: Percentage of Tested *Escherichia* (*E.*) *co li* and *Listeria* Samples Submitted to CDC's PulseNet within 4 Working Days

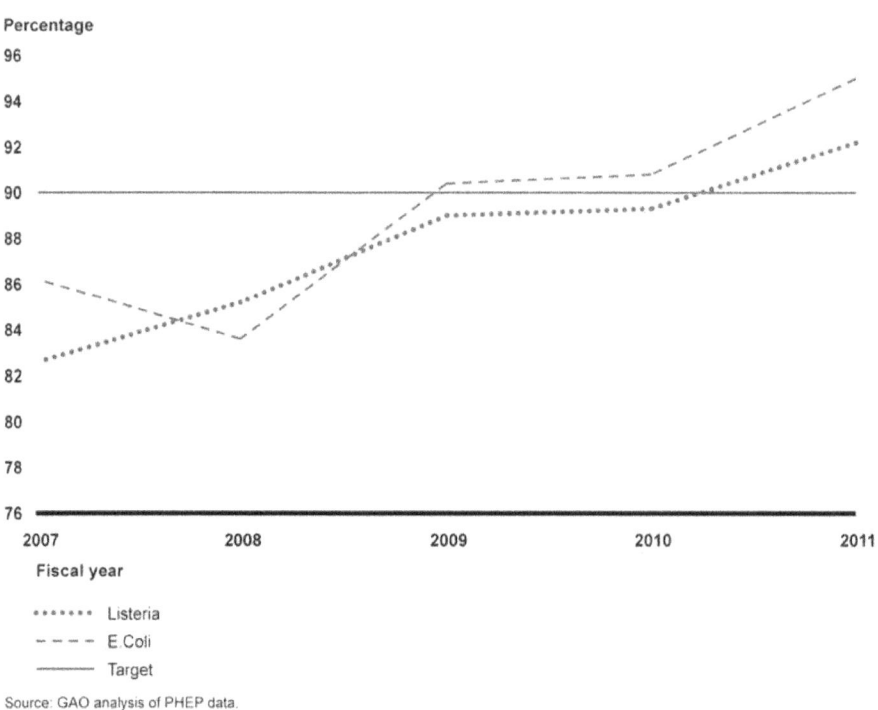

Percentage

... Listeria
- - - - E.Coli
——— Target

Source: GAO analysis of PHEP data.

Awardees also showed improvement over time for the performance measure on staff notification from 2007 through 2010.[58] For this performance measure, the time for appropriate response staff members to acknowledge that they received notification of a public health emergency increased from an average of 85 minutes to 971 minutes (16.2 hours) from fiscal year 2007 through fiscal year 2008; however, performance steadily improved from fiscal year 2008 through fiscal year

---

[58]CDC discontinued staff notification as a performance measure in 2011.

GAO-13-278 Medical and Public Health Preparedness

2010, decreasing to 53 minutes in fiscal year 2010.[59] However, the percentage of incidents in which awardees' staff members took 1 hour or less to respond to a staff notification decreased slightly from an average of 91 percent for all awardees in fiscal year 2007 to 87 percent in 2010. (See fig. 2.) CDC officials said that a majority of outliers identified during the agency's data validation processes were due to documentation problems, such as one awardee taking more than 500 hours to notify staff during an emergency in fiscal year 2008, resulting in an average of 16.2 hours for all awardees. These problems can be a result of awardees not documenting stop times for performance measure activities or misunderstanding the question stated in the CDC data collection database, CDC officials said. In these cases, CDC provides technical assistance to awardees. For example, because of some documentation problems, CDC now distributes a tool to help awardees correctly document the start and stop times for the staff notification and staff assembly activities. In addition, CDC officials said that they ask awardees that report longer notification periods to retest their performance for this activity in the first 6 months of the next fiscal year.

[59]We calculated staff notification times for all incidents, including both exercises and real events that awardees reported in a given fiscal year. For example, in fiscal year 2010, we calculated staff notification times for a total of 125 incidents. The number of incidents exceeds the number of awardees because in many cases, awardees reported more than one incident per year. For example, one awardee reported staff notification times for four incidents.

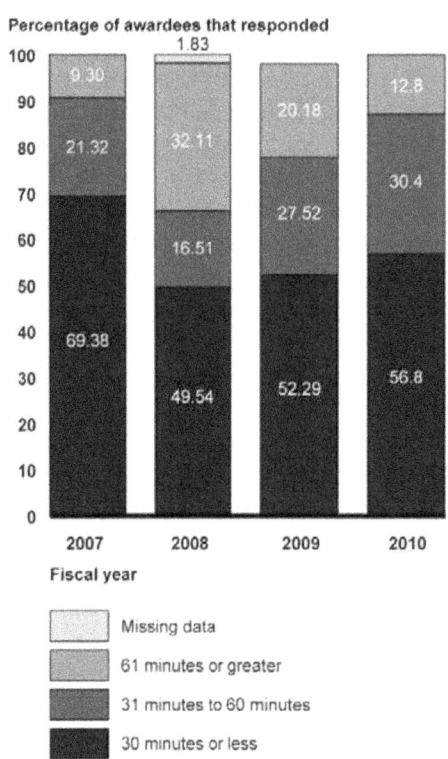

Figure 2: Awardee Response Times for Performance Measure on Staff Notification, Fiscal Year 2007 through Fiscal Year 2010

Percentage of awardees that responded

Fiscal year

Missing data

61 minutes or greater

31 minutes to 60 minutes

30 minutes or less

Source: GAO analysis of PHEP data.

For the performance measure on staff assembly, the time for appropriate response staff to assemble increased from 35 minutes to 72 minutes (1.2 hours) from fiscal year 2007 through fiscal year 2008; however, from fiscal year 2008 through fiscal year 2011, performance steadily improved, decreasing from an average of 72 minutes (1.2 hours) to an average of 31 minutes. But the percentage of awardees whose staff members took 1 hour or less to respond varied: 82 percent of awardees were able to respond in 1 hour or less in fiscal year 2007, 64 percent in fiscal year 2008, 85 percent in fiscal year 2009, 84 percent in fiscal year 2010, and 95 percent in 2011. (See fig. 3.) Beginning in 2009, CDC designated a 60-minute performance target for the 50 state awardees only; in fiscal year 2011, state awardees were able to respond in 60 minutes or less 95 percent of the time.

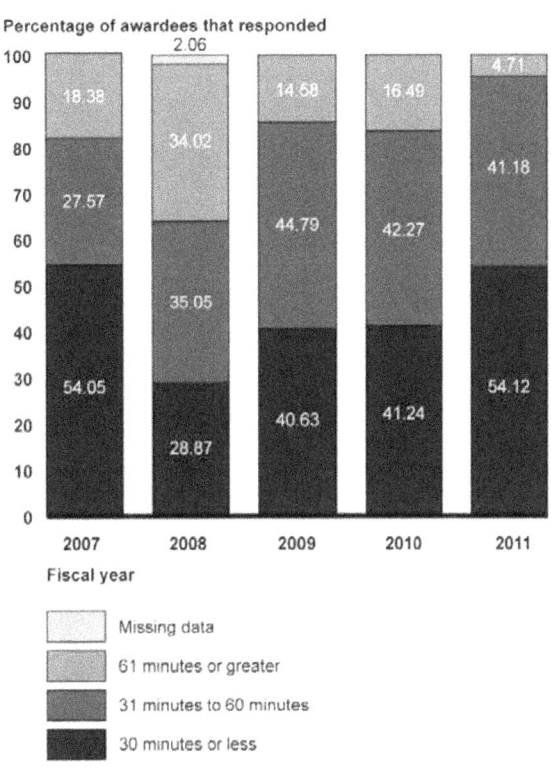

Figure 3: Awardee Response Times for Performance Measure on Staff Assembly, Fiscal Year 2007 through Fiscal Year 2011

Percentage of awardees that responded

Fiscal year

Missing data

61 minutes or greater

31 minutes to 60 minutes

30 minutes or less

Source: GAO analysis of PHEP data.

Although awardees showed improvement in the staff notification and staff assembly performance measure activities on average over time, the reported times for these activities varied greatly across awardees within individual fiscal years. For example, in fiscal year 2011, while half of the awardees reported being able to assemble public health emergency response staff within 30 minutes, the time it took for individual awardees to assemble staff ranged from 2 minutes to 90 minutes, with a majority of awardees clustered between 2 and 60 minutes. (See fig. 4.)

GAO-13-278 Medical and Public Health Preparedness

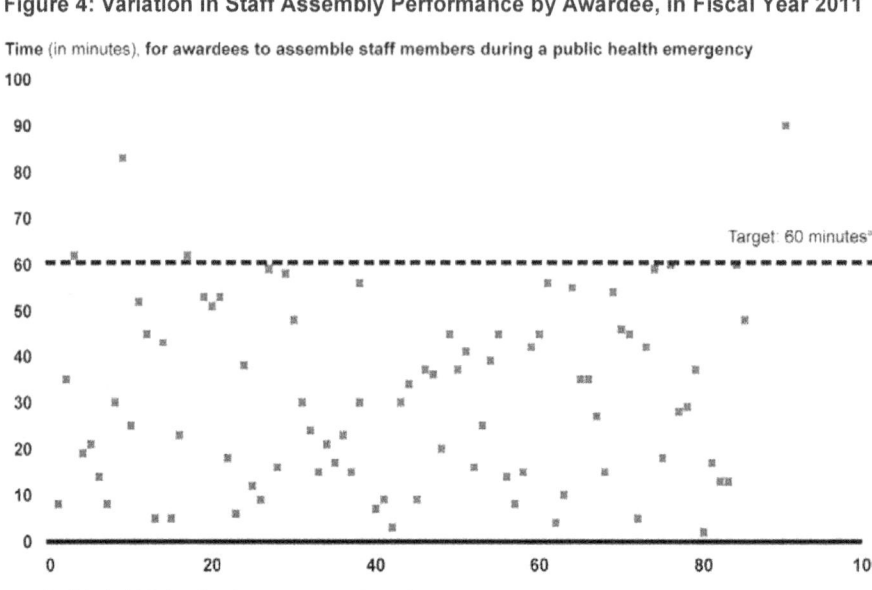

Figure 4: Variation in Staff Assembly Performance by Awardee, in Fiscal Year 2011

Time (in minutes), for awardees to assemble staff members during a public health emergency

Incidents (drill, functional exercise, or real event)

Source: GAO analysis of PHEP data.

[a]The 60-minute performance target applies to the 50 state awardees only.

For three of the remaining performance measures—incident action plan, after-action report and improvement plan, and emergency response communication—awardees' performance was generally steady or declined. For the performance measure on the incident action plan, awardees' performance remained roughly the same from fiscal year 2007 through fiscal year 2011, with 96 to 98 percent of awardees able to develop an incident action plan within CDC's designated time frame. For the performance measure on after-action report and improvement plan, the time it took for awardees to develop an after-action report following a public health emergency varied. For example, awardees took an average of 34 days to develop an after-action report in fiscal year 2007, 46 days in 2008, 56 days in 2009, 43 days in 2010, and 47 days in 2011. For the performance measure on emergency response communication—the time to develop emergency messages for the public—performance declined in the first 4 years of our study period and improved in the last year. In fiscal year 2010, it took awardees an average of 943 minutes (15.7 hours) to develop a message—almost 9 hours longer than the fiscal year 2008 average of 407 minutes (6.8 hours). Awardees showed improvement in fiscal year 2011, developing emergency messages for the public in an average of 348 minutes (5.8 hours).

CDC also collected data for 26 other performance measures during fiscal years 2007 and 2011, but the agency had these measures in place for only 1 year. These 26 performance measures provide data on five preparedness activities: awardees' ability to contact key response partners in an emergency in case of power outages, plan for and exercise the distribution of medical materiel and dispensing of medical countermeasures, perform public health surveillance and epidemiological investigations, perform additional public health laboratory testing, and prepare communities. CDC did not include contacting key response partners as a performance measure after 2007 and only designated the 25 other performance measures in 2011.[60] From fiscal year 2007 through fiscal year 2010, CDC scored awardees' performance in planning for and carrying out distribution and dispensing activities, including designating a minimum target score using a specific scoring tool designed for these activities, but CDC did not designate a specific performance measure.[61] CDC officials told us that the agency's scoring methodology was not originally intended to serve as an indicator of awardee performance but rather to assess the level of awardees' planning and determine the need for technical assistance. However, beginning in 2011, CDC developed a new composite measure and score for medical countermeasure dispensing and medical materiel management and distribution for fiscal year 2011 and beyond that officials believe better represents awardee preparedness for these activities.

---

[60]Because CDC collected only 1 year of data on these measures, we were unable to identify trends in performance across years and therefore did not analyze awardee data for these measures.

[61]Because CDC did not have a performance measure for countermeasure distribution and dispensing for most of our study period, and because CDC conducted its own analysis of awardee scores across fiscal years and updated the analysis annually, we did not analyze awardee performance for this activity. According to the agency's analysis, awardees generally met the annual minimum target score of 79 or higher in fiscal years 2009 and 2010, scoring an average of 88 in those years. See Centers for Disease Control and Prevention, *Public Health Preparedness: 2011 State-by-State Update on Laboratory Capabilities and Response Readiness Planning* (Washington, D.C.: September 2011).

CDC Lacks Performance Targets to Effectively Assess Awardee Progress toward Meeting the PHEP Public Health Preparedness Goal

According to CDC officials, the agency reviews awardee-submitted data annually in order to gauge the progress of its awardees in carrying out PHEP performance measure activities to meet the PHEP goal, and it provides technical assistance to awardees when necessary. However, from fiscal years 2007 through 2011, CDC lacked a comprehensive performance management system that included both performance measures that remained consistent over time and performance targets for each measure. Our prior work has shown that a system of performance measures with corresponding targets is important for assessing progress toward specified goals.[62] During fiscal years 2007 through 2011, CDC added some performance measures and dropped others and developed associated targets that were used for more than 1 year for only two measures. In addition, by 2011 CDC had developed only four performance targets for any of the measures. In contrast, the agency has set performance targets and interim milestones in other areas. For example, for medical materiel and countermeasure distribution and dispensing activities, CDC has designated what we consider performance targets for awardees and Cities Readiness Initiative (CRI) jurisdictions, a subset of PHEP. For these activities, CDC established a minimum recommended target score for acceptable performance, and it has increased this score incrementally throughout the life of the program. CDC officials stated that incremental increases in awardee and CRI jurisdiction scores were designed to provide a new target for states and localities so that they could continue to receive technical assistance tailored to their level of performance to improve in these activities. However, most of the PHEP measures CDC currently uses to assess awardee progress remain without targets, making it difficult to fully evaluate awardee progress.

CDC officials told us that in previous years, the agency did not specify performance targets for certain measures because the data showed too much variation across awardees. CDC officials acknowledged that without performance targets they have only been able to track awardee trends in performance over time. The officials noted that tracking awardee trends across years and drawing conclusions about why awardee performance in certain areas might vary from year to year are difficult because different types of events may require different types of responses. For example, according to officials, response needs for events

---

[62]GAO/T-GGD/AIMD-95-187.

like infectious disease outbreaks cannot be compared to those for natural disasters, and even comparing response needs for one type of natural disaster to those for another can be problematic. However, the PHEP cooperative agreement is intended to build all-hazards preparedness and response capabilities and by design does not focus on preparedness by event type. For example, the time it takes CDC or a state to determine that a public health emergency is occurring may depend on the type of event, but the time it takes to notify preidentified staff with incident management responsibilities should not depend on the type of event once the event is acknowledged.

The 15 capabilities outlined in CDC's 2011 *Public Health Preparedness Capabilities: National Standards for State and Local Planning* provide a new organizing framework and new performance measures for PHEP awardees' public health preparedness activities for fiscal year 2011 and beyond, but the agency still lacks a comprehensive performance management system with objective, quantifiable, and measureable targets tied to the new performance measures that would allow CDC to assess awardee progress in meeting the PHEP goal.[63] CDC released 47 performance measures for 14 of the 15 new public health capabilities for fiscal year 2012 but has developed corresponding performance targets for only 4 of these measures.[64] CDC officials told us that basing performance on detailed capabilities derived from national and strategic priorities for preparedness and response rather than on performance measures developed using subject-matter expert, awardee, and other stakeholder input has made it easier to define performance measures.

---

[63]Centers for Disease Control and Prevention, *Public Health Preparedness Capabilities: National Standards for State and Local Planning* (Washington, D.C.: March 2011). The 15 public health capabilities are community preparedness, community recovery, emergency operations coordination, emergency public information and warning, fatality management, information sharing, mass care, medical countermeasure dispensing, medical materiel management and distribution, medical surge, public health laboratory testing, public health surveillance and epidemiological investigation, nonpharmaceutical interventions, responder safety and health, and volunteer management.

[64]Seventeen of the 47 measures are new for fiscal year 2012. The 14 capabilities may have more than one associated performance measure. For example, the community preparedness capability has four corresponding performance measures: identification of key organizations, community engagement in risk identification, community engagement in public health preparedness activities, and community engagement in recovery planning. For the remaining capability, CDC developed an evaluation tool to assess awardee progress but did not specify any performance measures. The new performance measures also include one joint HPP-PHEP measure.

The shift to a capabilities-based approach in 2011 provided CDC with a foundation on which to build performance metrics, whereas prior to 2011, developing PHEP metrics was difficult, officials said. However, CDC considers the new PHEP measures developed in 2011 for fiscal year 2012 to be provisional. Although CDC has been collecting data on PHEP activities since 2002 and implemented its first set of performance measures in 2006, CDC officials told us that they were collecting baseline data to help inform development of performance targets for applicable measures, including those that had been in place prior to fiscal year 2012. In addition, CDC is currently evaluating the performance measures to determine whether the agency will retain, modify, or discontinue them. According to officials, CDC plans to complete this evaluation in May 2013 and will continue to periodically review performance measures to ensure that they remain relevant and useful for program improvement and accountability, consistent with GPRAMA's emphasis on the importance of performance measures for assessing program performance.[65] However, in commenting on a draft of this report, agency officials estimated that it could take up to 3 years for CDC to fully establish targets and finalize the new performance measures for the 15 public health capabilities. Our prior work found that sustaining improvement requires ongoing performance measurement to identify new needs and opportunities to make further improvements.[66] By having only four performance targets at the start of the 2012 project cycle and provisional performance measures for fiscal year 2012 that are still subject to change in subsequent years, CDC may have created a system that will not allow the agency to fully assess awardee progress in 2012 and beyond or determine whether progress made in the new project cycle builds on progress made in prior cycles.

---

[65]Pub. L. No. 111-352, § 3, 124 Stat. 3867 (2011) (pertinent provision codified at 31 U.S.C. § 1115(b)).

[66]GAO/T-GGD/AIMD-95-187.

HHS Uses Internal Databases, Site Visits, and Audit Reports to Help Awardees Meet Requirements

HHS helps awardees meet cooperative agreement requirements by using internal databases, site visits, and audit reports to monitor their activities and identify the need for technical assistance. Officials from ASPR and CDC said that they use several different internal databases to ensure awardee compliance with application renewal and reporting requirements.[67] From these databases, ASPR and CDC can generate reports on the progress of each awardee in meeting application renewal and reporting deadlines and identify those awardees in need of technical assistance. For example, ASPR officials told us that ASPR's project officers begin to monitor awardees' progress in completing their reports about 60 days before the reporting deadline, in addition to regular, year-round monitoring. They continue to generate spreadsheets that track awardee reporting progress and send reminder notices as the reporting deadline approaches. In addition, the officials said that their databases can lock out or prevent awardees from submitting renewal applications and midyear and end-of-year progress reports after the deadline.[68]

ASPR and CDC officials said they use internal databases to monitor awardee compliance with the matching and maintenance of funding requirements of HPP and PHEP awards. Through these databases, ASPR and CDC review application information and federal financial reports submitted by awardees to determine whether awardees are in compliance with HPP and PHEP matching and maintenance of funds requirements.[69] For example, CDC officials told us that in 2010, the agency began developing technical assistance plans to monitor matching and maintenance of funds requirements. After an awardee has submitted an application and a completed budget that identifies potential sources of matching funds, this information is incorporated into the technical

---

[67]ASPR and CDC use HHS's payment management database to monitor awardee expenditures. In addition, for fiscal year 2012, both ASPR and CDC began using CDC's database to monitor application, financial, and reporting requirements. ASPR and CDC officials said they are working in conjunction with HHS's Administration for Children and Families to develop an enhanced program, performance, and fiscal management information technology system for 2014.

[68]According to ASPR and CDC officials, cases in which awardees are unable to meet reporting deadlines are typically a result of a public health emergency such as Hurricane Katrina or the 2010 oil spill in the Gulf of Mexico. In such cases, awardees may request a deadline extension.

[69]As of 2011, ASPR awardees were required to submit their maintenance of funding plan within 30 days of receiving their award if such a plan was not included in the initial application.

assistance plan.[70] CDC officials said that they use these plans to help ensure that awardees meet matching requirements and to assist them with handling in-kind donations, identifying partners, establishing fair market values for donations, and validating costs. CDC monitors the awardees' progress in carrying out activities in the technical assistance plan on a quarterly basis. Both ASPR and CDC officials told us that there has not been an instance in which an awardee was not able to meet the matching requirement. ASPR and CDC officials said that if such a case should occur, the awardee would have its HPP or PHEP funds reduced by the amount of the match it was unable to meet. To address maintenance of funds requirements, ASPR and CDC review awardees' maintenance of funding plans to ensure that awardees' expenditures are equal to or greater than those in the preceding 2-year reporting period.

ASPR and CDC also query the databases regularly to review financial information and reports and compare awardee expenditures with proposed budgets and work plans submitted with their applications to help ensure that awardees are meeting requirements for the appropriate use of HPP and PHEP funds. ASPR officials said they generate semi-annual and annual cash management disbursement reports and progress reports that show how awardees are spending funds. Since fiscal year 2009, ASPR has collected information on expenditures by preparedness activity in midyear and end-of-year reports to determine whether awardees met financial requirements. Officials from both ASPR and CDC told us that if they find that an awardee has misused HPP or PHEP funds, they report the awardee to HHS's Office of the Inspector General (OIG). The awardee may be required to complete a corrective action plan and reimburse the agency for the misused portion of its grant funds. ASPR and CDC officials also monitor awardee activity to determine whether they should provide technical assistance in meeting financial requirements. For example, ASPR officials told us that they use data collected from midyear reports to determine whether awardees are having trouble meeting requirements for spending or obligating funds and therefore need technical assistance.

---

[70]CDC officials said that awardees may request extensions when they have difficulty identifying financial sources for matching fund requirements.

In addition to using internal databases, ASPR and CDC help ensure awardee compliance with cooperative agreement requirements through site visits and by reviewing state and federal audit reports. ASPR and CDC conduct site visits at awardee locations to examine programmatic and financial activities. ASPR officials said that in the past they aimed to conduct site visits at each awardee location every 18 months, and CDC officials said they conducted site visits every 2 to 3 years. Beginning in fiscal year 2012, however, officials said that ASPR and CDC have scheduled joint site visits at HPP and PHEP awardee locations to take place every 12 to 18 months. CDC officials said they choose which sites to visit on the basis of a priority list that orders visits by (1) awardees that did not receive a visit in the prior year, (2) awardees that have issues that need to be addressed, and (3) the date of the most recent visit. In addition to information from databases and site visits, ASPR and CDC also review state and federal audit reports, such as single annual (A-133) audits, and other awardee information to determine whether awardees are compliant with financial requirements.[71]

ASPR and CDC require awardees that have problems managing their HPP and PHEP funds to complete a corrective action plan and then monitor these awardees' progress in addressing the issues outlined in the plan; in some cases, ASPR and CDC also restrict awardees' access to their funds. For example, in 2010, ASPR restricted an awardee's use of its HPP funds by requiring it to seek approval from ASPR for each withdrawal of funds for program-related activities after determining that the awardee had not adequately documented its request to use HPP funds for travel and personnel expenses.[72] ASPR also required the

---

[71]Awardees may submit the results of their A-133 audits in lieu of the biennial audit provided they include their HPP and PHEP expenditures in the audit. According to ASPR and CDC officials, since the biennial audit requirement went into effect in 2007, all awardees have chosen to submit A-133 audits to fulfill this requirement. HHS OIG reviews the A-133 audit results, issues notification letters to awardees if problems were identified during the audit, and reports audit findings to the operating division within HHS that funded the program.

[72]During fiscal years 2007 through 2011, ASPR determined that 11 of the 62 awardees had problems managing their HPP funds, including using funds to pay for unallowable expenses and not paying HPP-related expenses during the period of funding availability. ASPR also told us that two awardees were reported to HHS OIG for suspected misuse of funds. In one case, the awardee worked with ASPR officials to resolve the issue. In the other case, a 2011 state OIG report found that an HPP subawardee inappropriately used $7,500 in HPP funds for training and equipment, although the funds were to be used only for exercises related to mass casualty events. ASPR referred the awardee to HHS OIG in February 2012, and the case was still pending as of March 2013.

GAO-13-278 Medical and Public Health Preparedness

awardee to complete a corrective action plan outlining the steps the awardee must take to be released from the restriction on its funds. The plan required the awardee to revise its HPP budget plan, attend workshops and training sessions, and develop administrative procedures for managing equipment items and vehicles used for program purposes. ASPR also worked with the awardee to revise its budget plan. In April 2012, ASPR rescinded its restriction on the awardee's use of its HPP funds. In another instance, CDC restricted an awardee's access to its funds for 6 years, starting in 2005, based on concerns about the awardee's ability to meet the programmatic and fiscal requirements of the cooperative agreement, including issues such as the awardee not obligating more than $16,000 in PHEP funds within the period funds were available under the cooperative agreement.[73] Since then, CDC has provided the awardee with technical assistance to help it make significant changes to its internal control processes and come into good standing with the PHEP requirements. In December 2011, CDC released the restriction placed on the awardee's funds.

Conclusions

Given the importance of preparing for large-scale public health emergencies that could quickly strain medical and public health resources and severely delay critical medical services for affected individuals, determining the level of state and local medical and public health preparedness for these emergencies is vital for appropriately allocating awardee resources to fill preparedness gaps. As a result, HHS would benefit from enhancing its HPP and PHEP performance management systems to better assess the effect of the cooperative agreements on awardee preparedness. Although ASPR and CDC have been able to see some trends in how awardees are carrying out HPP and PHEP activities over time, creating comprehensive performance management systems with realistic targets and incremental milestones would allow them to

[73]During fiscal years 2007 through 2011, CDC determined that 14 of the 62 awardees had problems managing their PHEP funds. In 2009, HHS OIG identified an awardee that used more than $323,000 of its PHEP base award funds to pay for pandemic influenza activities rather than funds received for that purpose under a pandemic influenza supplemental appropriation. Because the awardee did not provide documentation to support the allowability of these funds, CDC instructed the awardee to reimburse the agency for the amount of PHEP funds in question. According to CDC officials, the awardee appealed the decision, which CDC denied. CDC officials also told us that the awardee has the option of escalating the case to HHS's Departmental Appeals Board. See Department of Health and Human Services, Office of the Inspector General, A-04-08-00047 (Washington, D.C.: November 2009).

more accurately gauge awardee performance and progress toward meeting the performance measures for the new health care and public health capabilities and the overall HPP and PHEP goals. Establishing these targets and milestones would also provide awardees with the ability to evaluate their own efforts to meet HPP and PHEP goals as they work through the 5-year project cycle that began in fiscal year 2012. Since ASPR and CDC use performance information to target technical assistance, performance management systems with targets and incremental milestones would also enable HHS to better direct that assistance to help awardees meet HPP and PHEP program goals and more effectively carry out activities to respond to public health emergencies. In addition, as the HPP and PHEP programs continue to grow and change, HHS would also benefit from ensuring that performance measures and targets remain consistent for a sufficient amount of time to capture this evolution. Adhering to a specific set of measures and targets for a fixed period would provide ASPR and CDC with the stability to better gauge whether awardees are meeting or making progress toward meeting short- and long-term preparedness goals.

Recommendations for Executive Action

To help ensure that HHS is adequately and comprehensively assessing HPP and PHEP awardees' performance and progress in meeting the medical and public health preparedness goals of the cooperative agreements, we recommend that the Secretary of Health and Human Services direct ASPR and CDC to take the following two actions:

- Develop objective and quantifiable performance targets and incremental milestones that correspond to the new HPP and PHEP performance measures, against which HHS can gauge progress toward the medical and public health preparedness goals of the cooperative agreements and direct technical assistance, as needed.

- Ensure that performance measures and targets remain consistent across the 5-year project cycle and that any future measures be comparable to determine whether awardees are making progress toward meeting short- and long-term medical and public health preparedness goals of the cooperative agreements.

Agency Comments and Our Evaluation

We provided a draft of this report to HHS, and its comments are reprinted in appendix IV. In its comments, HHS agreed with both of our recommendations but indicated that it would not be able to fully implement them for up to 3 years. HHS concurred with our first recommendation that it develop objective and quantifiable performance targets and incremental milestones. However, HHS stated that it would take until fiscal year 2016 to assess the validity, utility, and reliability of its current measures, after which it would develop associated targets. For example, in fiscal years 2014 and 2015, HHS plans to develop incremental milestones tied to HPP performance measures and targets based on fiscal year 2012 data. In the interim, HHS stated that it will take steps to develop preliminary targets and adjust them incrementally based on new data. We recognize that the development of evidence-based performance measures and targets is a process that requires substantial agency time and work. However, as we state in the report, HHS has been collecting data on state and local medical and public health preparedness activities since 2002 and has had a variety of performance measures in place since at least as early as 2006. In addition, the activities awardees are to conduct with HPP and PHEP funding have not changed substantially in more than 5 years. We encourage HHS to use data it has collected over the long term, in addition to the data collected under the new performance measures, to develop reasonable, objective, and quantifiable performance targets more expeditiously to provide HPP and PHEP awardees with some guidance as to HHS's performance expectations.

HHS concurred with our second recommendation that HPP and PHEP performance measures and targets remain consistent across the programs' current 5-year period. However, HHS stated that it may not be able to implement final performance measures for the full project cycle because its validation of the current provisional measures could take up to 3 years to complete, and it added that it would continue to change measures as needed. For example, HHS stated that some of the current 47 PHEP performance measures—25 of which were new for fiscal year 2011 and 17 of which were new for fiscal year 2012—would be dropped or modified and new measures added based on the department's evaluation within the next 3 years. We support HHS efforts to streamline the performance measures and potentially reduce the number of measures so as to reduce awardee burden. However, we are concerned that not finalizing the measures until the end of the current project cycle would lead to continued inconsistencies in both awardee expectations and performance assessment. We urge HHS to work more quickly to finalize these measures using new and previously collected data and stakeholder input. We also urge HHS to consider how it will use or build upon finalized measures in future project cycles without making wholesale changes to its performance measures.

HHS also provided information about its reporting on awardee progress since 2008 and its efforts to align and enhance the HPP and PHEP programs, to invest in science-based measurement capabilities, and to implement a joint ASPR and CDC information technology system to help manage HPP and PHEP. For example, HHS provided information on an exercise measurement tool it developed to help hospitals and health care coalitions to identify challenges in responding to a mass casualty event with no notice. In addition, HHS provided technical comments, which we incorporated as appropriate.

We are sending a copy of this report to the Secretary of Health and Human Services. In addition, the report is available at no charge on the GAO website at http://www.gao.gov.

If you or your staffs have any questions about this report, please contact me at (202) 512-7114 or crossem@gao.gov. Contact points for our Offices of Congressional Relations and Public Affairs may be found on the last page of this report. Key contributors to this report are listed in appendix V.

Marcia Crosse
Director, Health Care

GAO-13-278 Medical and Public Health Preparedness

Appendix I: Medical Surge Preparedness

Emergency preparedness experts agree that a natural disaster, infectious disease outbreak, or intentional terrorist attack that results in mass casualties could quickly overwhelm hospitals and public health systems and severely delay the delivery of critical medical services. In mass casualty emergencies, hospitals and health care facilities would need the ability to "surge"—that is, to have the staff, resources, and equipment in place to adequately care for increased numbers of affected individuals or individuals with unusual or highly specialized needs. Medical surge preparedness includes planning for the likelihood that individual hospitals would use existing systems that typically provide daily medical care to respond to public health emergencies and thus experience staffing and equipment shortages and require assistance with these and other resources, along with support from area hospitals and health care facilities and the surrounding community, and may need to care for patients at alternate sites.[1] Federal, state, and local public health agencies also play a role in medical surge, such as tracking and predicting disease outbreaks to develop response strategies; providing clinicians, laboratorians, public health officials, and the public with guidance and information on illness and injury prevention, treatment, and control, and shelter-in-place strategies to help ensure individuals seek care in appropriate settings; and providing medical countermeasures through federal and state caches.[2]

Depending on the type of public health emergency, affected individuals would arrive at health care facilities with different types of illness or injury over different time frames. In a mass casualty event such as a natural disaster or an intentional detonation of a conventional explosive or a

---

[1]Alternate care sites can be fixed or mobile facilities set up to care for individuals affected by a public health emergency when hospitals exceed capacity. Alternate care sites can be used to deliver medical care outside hospital settings and conduct triage to determine which patients need critical attention and immediate transport to the hospital and which have less serious injuries. Fixed facilities are buildings that because of their size or proximity to a hospital can be adapted to provide medical care. Mobile facilities are either specialized units with surgical and intensive care capabilities on tractor-trailer platforms or fully equipped hospitals stored in containers that can be set up quickly.

[2]Medical countermeasures include drugs, vaccines, and devices to diagnose, treat, prevent, or mitigate potential effects of exposure to harmful agents, such as biological pathogens or chemicals. The Centers for Disease Control and Prevention (CDC) maintains the Strategic National Stockpile, the national repository of medications, medical supplies, and equipment for use in a public health emergency.

radiological dispersal device,[3] affected individuals would be likely to sustain serious to minor physical trauma—blunt or penetrating injuries ranging from serious eye injuries, burns, and lacerations to sprains, strains, and minor wounds—and would be likely to arrive at a hospital within minutes to hours after the event. In a mass casualty event such as an influenza pandemic, an intentional release of a biological agent such as anthrax, or an emerging infectious disease outbreak, affected individuals may become ill and, in the case of transmissible disease, expose family, friends, and other contacts to illness. Depending on the severity of illness and the time it takes to develop symptoms, these individuals may arrive at a health care facility such as a doctor's office, a community-based or urgent care center, or a hospital emergency department within hours to days of exposure. To accommodate these individuals, hospitals could cancel elective admissions or discharge patients who no longer need critical care or transfer them to other facilities; however, hospitals may not be able to discharge or transfer patients in intensive care units. Furthermore, even with adequate physical space, hospitals may not have clinicians available who have the specialized skills or knowledge to treat penetrating wounds and burns or to diagnose and treat rare or emerging diseases.[4]

Mass casualty events would exacerbate the crowding and staff shortages that many hospital emergency departments and trauma centers currently experience in nonemergency periods and that can negatively affect access to and quality of care or delay needed treatment. The Centers for Disease Control and Prevention (CDC) estimates that about 136 million people visited hospital emergency departments in 2009 (the most recent year for which data are available), with about 45 million, or 33 percent, of

---

[3]A radiological dispersal device, or "dirty bomb," is a mix of explosives, such as dynamite, with radioactive material. When the dynamite or other explosives are set off, the blast carries radioactive material into the surrounding area.

[4]In the case of an infectious disease outbreak, hospitals would also need to help prevent the spread of disease by airborne pathogens by placing infected individuals in negative pressure isolation rooms and having available appropriate equipment and supplies to treat patients and health care workers.

these visits the result of physical trauma.[5] Hospital emergency departments in many cities[6] have problems handling the volume of patients resulting from a multiple-car highway crash, let alone the numbers of individuals who could become ill or be injured in a mass casualty public health emergency.[7] In its 2007 publication on hospital-based emergency and trauma care, the Institute of Medicine (IOM) reported that 91 percent of rural and urban emergency departments said overcrowding was a problem, with 40 percent of emergency departments reporting overcrowding as a daily occurrence. Trauma centers in certain cities and regions have closed because of the high cost of care and high levels of uncompensated care,[8] and emergency departments and trauma centers face staffing shortages in key areas such as on-call specialists and trauma and critical care surgeons. Rural hospital emergency departments also face a number of problems that can lead to crowding and negatively affect patient care, such as fewer hospitals, limited availability of equipment, inadequate supply of qualified emergency and trauma clinicians, and long distances to hospitals, resulting in increased emergency response times. We previously reported on hospital

---

[5]Physical trauma is a blunt or penetrating injury or set of injuries. While most emergency departments can treat individuals with minor injuries, trauma centers are hospitals or specialized centers within hospitals that have the resources and equipment to help treat severely injured individuals. Trauma centers can be classified from Level I to Level IV based on the care they provide, with Level I trauma centers providing the highest level of care and Level IV centers providing initial trauma care and transfer to a higher-level trauma center if necessary.

[6]Approximately two-thirds of hospitals with emergency departments are located in metropolitan areas. In addition, most emergency department visits occurred in metropolitan hospitals. According to CDC, in 2009 about 111 million (or 81 percent) of the 136 million emergency department visits occurred in metropolitan hospitals, compared to about 25 million (or 19 percent) visits in nonmetropolitan areas. Metropolitan hospitals are located in metropolitan statistical areas. The Office of Management and Budget defines a metropolitan statistical area as a region with at least one urbanized area that has a population of at least 50,000 and comprises the central county or counties containing the core, plus adjacent outlying counties having a high degree of social and economic integration with the central county or counties as measured through commuting.

[7]Institute of Medicine, *Hospital-Based Emergency Care: At the Breaking Point* (Washington, D.C.: 2007).

[8]As a condition of participating in Medicare, hospitals with emergency departments and trauma centers are required to provide emergency care to all individuals who request it regardless of their ability to pay. *See* 42 U.S.C. § 1395dd.

emergency department crowding and found that crowding has continued to occur.[9]

Hospital emergency department overcrowding can be attributed to several factors. In 2007, IOM reported that the most common cause is boarding, a practice in which patients are held in the emergency department until an inpatient bed becomes available.[10] Other factors that may contribute to crowding include large numbers of uninsured individuals and Medicaid beneficiaries in any given city or region who lack or have limited access to community-based primary and specialty care and the growing severity of medical conditions in individuals who come to the emergency department for care. Our 2009 report found that indicators of crowding included boarding and two additional factors, ambulance diversion (hospitals asking ambulances to bypass their emergency departments and transport patients to other facilities) and wait times (the amount of time patients wait to see a physician compared to recommended time frames based on severity of illness or injury and total time spent in the emergency department).[11]

---

[9]See GAO, *Hospital Emergency Departments: Crowding Continues to Occur, and Some Patients Wait Longer than Recommended Time Frames*, GAO-09-347 (Washington, D.C.: Apr. 30, 2009), and *Hospital Emergency Departments: Crowded Conditions Vary among Hospitals and Communities*, GAO-03-460 (Washington, D.C.: Mar. 14, 2003).

[10]Lack of available inpatient beds may be due to competition between emergency department admissions and scheduled hospital admissions such as those for elective surgical procedures. Hospitals may consider scheduled admissions for surgical procedures such as joint replacement to be more profitable than emergency department admissions for medical conditions such as pneumonia and may reserve inpatient beds for elective admissions.

[11]GAO-09-347.

Appendix II: Hospital Preparedness Program (HPP) Performance Measures, Fiscal Years 2007 and 2008

Performance measures (by preparedness element)	2007	2008
Communications systems		
• Number of participating hospitals that demonstrated dedicated, redundant communications during an exercise or event, as evidenced by exercise evaluations or after-action reports	✓+ Target: 75 percent	✓+ Target: 100 percent
• Number of participating hospitals that have demonstrated two-way communications capability with the Incident Command and health care coalition partners during an exercise or event, as evidenced by exercise evaluations or after-action reports	✓+ Target: 50 percent	✓+ Target: 100 percent
Education and training		
• Number of participating hospitals that have identified appropriate personnel for training and verified completion of specific training		✓+ Target: 100 percent
Emergency medical volunteers		
• Number of awardees able to generate a list of volunteer health professionals by category within 2 hours of a Department of Health and Human Services (HHS) or other request	✓+ Target: 50 percent	✓+ Target: 60 percent
• Number of awardees able to submit a verified list of volunteer health professionals within 8 hours of an HHS or other request	✓+ Target: 50 percent	
• Number of awardees able to compile an initial list of volunteer health professionals by discipline and credential level, within 12 hours of an HHS or other request		✓+ Target: 60 percent
• Number of awardees able to report a verified list of volunteer health professionals by discipline and credential level, within 24 hours of an HHS or other request		✓+ Target: 60 percent
Fatality management plans		
• Number of participating hospitals with mass fatality management plans		✓+ Target: 100 percent
Hospital bed availability		
• Number of awardees with state emergency operations centers able to report available beds for at least 75 percent of participating hospitals to the HHS Secretary's Operations Center within 4 hours of a request, during an exercise or event	✓+ Target: 100 percent	✓+ Target: 100 percent
• The number of participating hospitals that can report available beds to the state emergency operations center within 60 minutes of a state request	✓+ Target: 75 percent	✓+ Target: 100 percent
Medical evacuation and shelter-in-place plans		
• Number of participating hospitals with medical evacuation plans		✓+ Target: 100 percent
National Incident Management System (NIMS)		
• The number of participating hospitals that incorporate NIMS concepts and principles for emergency events		✓+ Target: 100 percent
Preparedness exercises		
• Number of awardees able to conduct exercises that incorporate NIMS concepts and principles and include hospitals in the exercises		✓+ Target: 100 percent

Legend: ✓ = performance measures applicable; + = performance targets applicable.

Source: GAO analysis of HPP funding opportunity announcements, fiscal years 2007 and 2008.

Appendix III: Data for Hospital Preparedness Program (HPP) Preparedness Elements and Metrics, Fiscal Years 2007 through 2011

Preparedness element and metrics[a]	2007 Percentage (number)	2008 Percentage (number)	2009 Percentage (number)	2010 Percentage (number)	2011[b] Percentage (number)
Communications systems					
• Participating hospitals that demonstrated dedicated, redundant communications during an exercise or event	90.3% (4,643)	88.6% (4,751)	92.1% (4,975)	90.4% (4,912)	91.4% (4,893)
Decontamination					
• Ambulatory and nonambulatory patients that can be decontaminated by awardee within a 3-hour period	N/A (392,605)	N/A (442,532)	N/A (612,963)	N/A (477,596)	N/A (481,810)
Education and training					
• Participating hospitals that have identified appropriate personnel for training	N/A	84.5% (4,528)	85.7% (4,631)	89.6% (4,868)	92.2% (4,932)
• Participating hospitals that have verified completion of training by appropriate personnel	N/A	86.9% (4,661)	79.6% (4,298)	86.7% (4,713)	90.4% (4,837)
Emergency medical volunteers					
• Awardees that can generate a verified list of available volunteers registered in an Emergency System for Advance Registration of Volunteer Health Professionals (ESAR-VHP) system within 24 hours of a request being issued by a requesting body or HHS Secretary's Operations Center	N/A (55)	N/A (57)	N/A (58)	N/A (59)	N/A (61)
• Total ESAR-VHP volunteers registered by awardees	N/A (147,037)	N/A (155,020)	N/A (179,811)	N/A (194,135)	N/A (197,434)
Fatality management plans					
• Participating hospitals with mass fatality management plans	62.6% (3,219)	60.4% (3,239)	72.5% (3,915)	77.2% (4,199)	78.3% (4,189)
Hospital bed availability					
• Participating hospitals that are able to report bed availability to the state emergency operations center within 60 minutes of a request	91.7% (4,713)	90.6% (4,857)	90.1% (4,866)	88.7% (4,823)	87.6% (4,688)
• Awardees that are able to report bed availability to HHS Secretary's Operations Center or other federal partner within 4 hours of a request	N/A (60)	N/A (61)	N/A (60)	N/A (62)	N/A (61)
Isolation					
• Number of awardee subregions that can maintain patients in negative pressure isolation in emergency departments	96.6% (341)	84.3% (323)	92.5% (345)	92.0% (347)	94.2% (357)
• Number of awardee subregions that can maintain patients in negative pressure isolation in nonemergency-department settings	96.6% (341)	49.9% (191)	104.8% (391)	88.9% (335)	93.4% (354)
Laboratory referral					
• Hospital-based laboratory personnel trained in protocols for clinical sample referral to public health laboratories	N/A (23,795)	25.5% (32,931)	31.5% (43,995)	33.0% (45,921)	29.6% (42,268)

Preparedness element and metrics[a]	2007 Percentage (number)	2008 Percentage (number)	2009 Percentage (number)	2010 Percentage (number)	2011[b] Percentage (number)
Medical evacuation and shelter-in-place plans					
• Participating hospitals with evacuation and shelter-in-place plans	79.9% (4,109)	82.3% (4,411)	83.1% (4,487)	87.9% (4,779)	88.3% (4,728)
National Incident Management System (NIMS)					
• Participating hospitals that have adopted NIMS	91.1% (4,683)	83.6% (4,482)	89.6% (4,841)	93.2% (5,069)	87.9% (4,705)
Partnerships					
• Number of awardees with memorandums of understanding reported	N/D	N/A (59)	N/A (58)	N/A (60)	N/A (61)
Preparedness exercises					
• Participating hospitals that took part in an exercise/event	88.3% (4,542)	78.5% (4,211)	86.0% (4,647)	87.3% (4,748)	87.3% (4,673)
• Participating hospitals that developed written improvement plans based on after-action reports	77.3% (3,976)	65.6% (3,516)	74.8% (4,038)	78.8% (4,281)	73.7% (3,943)

Legend: N/A = not applicable, N/D = no data were collected.

Source: GAO analysis of ASPR end-of-year HPP data.

[a]Data collected for 2 of the 14 preparedness elements—"medical countermeasures" and "telecommunications service priority"—reflect a single count at a specific point in time and therefore could not be evaluated across our study period.

[b]Fiscal year 2011 numbers and percentages were calculated from unvalidated data. ASPR validates awardee-submitted data to help ensure accuracy of the information. ASPR had not yet completed its validation of the HPP data, which were due to ASPR September 30, 2012, by the time we completed our analysis in December 2012.

Appendix IV: Comments from the Department of Health and Human Services

DEPARTMENT OF HEALTH & HUMAN SERVICES | OFFICE OF THE SECRETARY

Assistant Secretary for Legislation
Washington, DC 20201

MAR 6

Marcia Crosse
Director, Health Care
U.S. Government Accountability Office
441 G Street NW
Washington, DC 20548

Dear Ms. Crosse:

Attached are comments on the U.S. Government Accountability Office's (GAO) report entitled, "NATIONAL PREPAREDNESS: Improvements Needed for Measuring Awardee Performance in Meeting Medical and Public Health Preparedness Goals" (GAO 13-278).

The Department appreciates the opportunity to review this report prior to publication.

Sincerely,

Jim R. Esquea
Assistant Secretary for Legislation

Attachment

GENERAL COMMENTS OF THE DEPARTMENT OF HEALTH AND HUMAN SERVICES (HHS) ON THE GOVERNMENT ACCOUNTABILITY OFFICE'S (GAO) DRAFT REPORT ENTITLED, "NATIONAL PREPAREDNESS: IMPROVEMENTS NEEDED FOR MEASURING AWARDEE PERFORMANCE IN MEETING MEDICAL AND PUBLIC HEALTH PREPAREDNESS GOALS" (GAO-13-278)

The Department appreciates the opportunity to review and comment on this draft report.

While our evaluation efforts have consistently evolved over the past decade, HHS has faced challenges in developing reliable, evidence-based performance measures and associated targets for the Public Health Emergency Preparedness (PHEP) program. Challenges include lack of a strong evidence base regarding public health preparedness and lack of consensus among the preparedness community on preparedness approaches. Despite these challenges, HHS has focused on accountability for the United States' preparedness investments. Since February 2008, HHS has published annual reports on the progress PHEP awardees have made since 2001 in disease detection and investigation, laboratory testing capabilities, and the planning, training, and exercising required to build emergency response capacities and capabilities.

HHS's release of the *Public Health Preparedness Capabilities: National Standards for State and Local Planning* in March 2011 represented a critical turning point for the PHEP program. This shift to a capabilities-based approach to public health preparedness provided an evidence-informed framework for developing performance measures. At that time, HHS recognized that the new capabilities model represented an opportunity to develop more robust performance measures with defined targets. Since then, HHS has worked diligently to establish the type of performance measurement system GAO recommends in its current draft report.

During the past two years, HHS has introduced into the field 40 of the current 47 PHEP performance measures and has started to validate the measures in terms of utility and relevance to awardees. At the end of this process, HHS expects to refine and reduce the measures and use the collected data to develop preliminary targets. HHS expects to release updated PHEP performance measure guidance, based on the results of its current performance measure evaluation project, by June 2013.

In 2012, the Hospital Preparedness Program (HPP) shifted its focus from hospital preparedness to health care system preparedness through building health care coalitions. HPP also defined eight foundational health care preparedness capabilities as the National Guidance for Healthcare System Preparedness. This pivotal change in direction resulted from the evolving discipline of healthcare preparedness, stakeholder input, and an evidence informed approach.

Performance targets and incremental milestones are very much a part of this shift to healthcare system preparedness. HPP is currently collecting baseline data from fiscal year (FY) 2012, which will inform all performance targets and incremental milestones for the five-year project period. Furthermore, HHS is pilot testing additional performance measures based on these new capabilities. HPP is refining the 2012 performance measures based on FY 2012 mid-year data (collected in January 2013) and input from key informants and stakeholder groups. Final FY 2013 performance measures will be released in June 2013 and will remain consistent and comparable through the project period. In fiscal years 2014 and 2015, HHS will continue to develop its performance management system by establishing incremental milestones tied to the finalized HPP performance measures. HPP will also quantify objective performance targets

1

**GENERAL COMMENTS OF THE DEPARTMENT OF HEALTH AND HUMAN
SERVICES (HHS) ON THE GOVERNMENT ACCOUNTABILITY OFFICE'S (GAO)
DRAFT REPORT ENTITLED, "NATIONAL PREPAREDNESS: IMPROVEMENTS
NEEDED FOR MEASURING AWARDEE PERFORMANCE IN MEETING MEDICAL
AND PUBLIC HEALTH PREPAREDNESS GOALS" (GAO-13-278)**

informed by evidence and science and linked to the eight healthcare preparedness capabilities.
These incremental milestones will allow HHS and other stakeholders to accurately monitor
awardee progress, track trends, and provide technical assistance where needed.

Advancing the Scientific Basis for Performance Measures

In 2011, Presidential Policy Directive #8 mandated measurement to determine progress toward
national preparedness goals. Unfortunately, investments in preparedness over the last decade
have significantly undervalued the need to build a science and evidence base for healthcare and
public health preparedness. As a result, the evidence base required to measure preparedness and
manage outcomes is severely deficient. As resources allow, HHS is making modest investments
in developing science-based measurement capabilities.

Over the last two years, HPP defined a set of core preparedness capabilities, discarded
inappropriate measures, and continues to develop and refine new capability-based performance
measures. As an example, HHS developed the Surge Stress Test, a standardized exercise
measurement tool for hospitals and health care coalitions. The Surge Stress Test allows health
systems to identify and understand the challenges of responding to a no-notice mass casualty
incident (MCI). The Surge Stress Test evaluates actions taken by hospitals and healthcare
coalitions to accommodate a large influx of casualties from a sudden, no-notice event. Actions
include efforts to create and more efficiently use space, staff, equipment, and other resources.
The aim is to produce a performance measurement linked assessment that can be widely adopted
and regularly used to support system improvement and accountability to external stakeholders.

Promoting Inter-Agency Coordination

An environment of strained resources requires greater coordination of preparedness efforts. To
that end, HHS began an intensive grant alignment effort in 2011 to improve coordination of
preparedness efforts between the PHEP program and HPP. In addition, the Office of the
Assistant Secretary for Preparedness and Response (ASPR) and Centers for Disease Control and
Prevention (CDC) co-developed joint performance measures which serve both programs and
focus on outcomes. These joint measures reflect the strategic intent to align HPP and PHEP
programs wherever possible.

ASPR co-developed and co-presented training with CDC on the joint performance measures for
HPP and PHEP awardees, and included the joint performance measures in each program's *FY
2012 Performance Measures Implementation Guidance*. The HPP and PHEP published their
respective *FY 2012 Performance Measures Implementation Guidance* with the same look and
feel to make them more user friendly to awardees. HPP and PHEP published their performance
measure documents on a single website (www.phe.gov) for ease of use. These efforts speak to
the larger discipline integration between public health and health care that can serve as a model
for other health efforts aimed at improved coordination.

2

**GENERAL COMMENTS OF THE DEPARTMENT OF HEALTH AND HUMAN
SERVICES (HHS) ON THE GOVERNMENT ACCOUNTABILITY OFFICE'S (GAO)
DRAFT REPORT ENTITLED, "NATIONAL PREPAREDNESS: IMPROVEMENTS
NEEDED FOR MEASURING AWARDEE PERFORMANCE IN MEETING MEDICAL
AND PUBLIC HEALTH PREPAREDNESS GOALS" (GAO-13-278)**

HHS agrees with GAO's comments on the current strains of the emergency care system and its
impact on preparedness and response activities. Within ASPR, the Emergency Care
Coordination Center (ECCC) promotes the alignment of federal programs, resources, and tools
that will improve the resiliency, efficiency, and effectiveness of our nation's emergency care. It
is important to recognize that the scope of the emergency care system extends across the entire
continuum of patient care: from the pre-hospital environment through the emergency department
and patient transfer or final disposition. Therefore multiple federal agencies are involved in the
oversight and management of the administration of emergency medical care.

Performance Measure Revisions in Budget Period 2

ASPR and CDC's joint five-year cooperative agreement began in 2012. During this project
period, HPP and PHEP are working to streamline evaluation processes, develop consistent
performance measures, coordinate training and guidance on performance measures to improve
data quality, improve their data capture, and track awardee progress.

Many of HPP's proposed changes are in line with GAO recommendations. The final
performance measures will be clearly linked to outcomes and will respond to multiple priorities.
The revised performance measures will be more targeted and will reduce the number of data
elements HPP collects from awardees.

At this time, HPP is adopting a framework to explore and validate appropriate methodologies
that will examine performance measures and determine their value. The project will be finalized
and published this year, and will establish a consistent set of performance measures and
accompanying data elements. The results of the project will inform how HPP implements
performance measures across awardees, how HPP develops new performance measures for
health care coalitions, and how HPP establishes performance benchmarks for each performance
measure. This will enhance continuous quality improvement, identify areas for targeted
performance improvement, and guide technical assistance and outreach activities. Based on the
results of this evidence-based approach, HPP may reduce some of its performance measures
and/or data elements through a process of psychometric testing, scaling, and factor analysis. The
reduction of unnecessary reporting will help HPP awardees focus on the requirements that are
most vital to medical and public health preparedness.

Utilizing Technology to Improve Awardee Monitoring

HHS recognizes that it is important to have a robust and consistent performance management
system that will allow ASPR and CDC to identify trends over time while streamlining the data
collection process to reduce the burden on awardees. Currently, ASPR and CDC have begun a
project to develop a comprehensive, modern information technology (IT) system that will reduce
awardee burden and better track and monitor federal investments. The IT system will be a joint
ASPR/CDC initiative to support the framework that HPP and PHEP have developed. This
framework will have the capability to integrate their program, evaluation, grants, and project

3

GENERAL COMMENTS OF THE DEPARTMENT OF HEALTH AND HUMAN
SERVICES (HHS) ON THE GOVERNMENT ACCOUNTABILITY OFFICE'S (GAO)
DRAFT REPORT ENTITLED, "NATIONAL PREPAREDNESS: IMPROVEMENTS
NEEDED FOR MEASURING AWARDEE PERFORMANCE IN MEETING MEDICAL
AND PUBLIC HEALTH PREPAREDNESS GOALS" (GAO-13-278)

management systems. The shared IT platform may result in significant cost savings in the long
term when compared to the current system being utilized by many awardees.

As resources are made available, the new platform will replace ASPR's current system with a
more effective performance management module and build a foundation for other program
management models. In later phases of the IT release, the new platform will update existing
work plan and budget models and will provide enhanced program management functionalities,
linking work plans to capabilities and budgets. In the final phase of the IT release, the new
system will replace tools and spreadsheets with more efficient awardee project management
tools, including formats for technical assistance planning and monitoring, a capabilities planning
guide and assessment, and sub-awardee tools for data collection. This final phase will integrate
grants management and program management modules. ASPR and CDC anticipate that they
will complete this work in 2015.

Path ahead: HPP Initiatives for FY2013

While research and experience in recent disasters have proved that the shift to capabilities is
critical in preparing communities for disasters, the science of health care preparedness is not
robust; developing the measurement tools and performance measures necessary to quantify an
effectively prepared health care system requires increased attention. HHS is committed to
ensuring the nation is prepared for a medical or public health disaster and will continue to refine
its performance measures and monitoring procedures according to the evolving science of
preparedness and the critical evidence it collects.

As discussed in FY 2013, as resources are made available, ASPR and CDC will collaborate to
support the implementation of a modern, user-friendly IT system that will improve data quality,
reduce burden of data entry for awardees, increase transparency of results, streamline reporting,
and facilitate the exchange of information among performance management, program
management, grants management officers, and awardees.

GAO Recommendation

GAO recommends that the Secretary of Health and Human Services direct ASPR and CDC to
develop objective and quantifiable performance targets and incremental milestones that
correspond to the new HPP and PHEP performance measures, against which HHS can gauge
progress toward the medical and public health preparedness goals of the cooperative agreements
and direct technical assistance as needed.

HHS Response

HHS concurs with GAO's first recommendation to develop objective and quantifiable
performance measures, including targets and incremental milestones, which are critical to
determining medical and public health preparedness on the national and local level. However, we

4

**GENERAL COMMENTS OF THE DEPARTMENT OF HEALTH AND HUMAN
SERVICES (HHS) ON THE GOVERNMENT ACCOUNTABILITY OFFICE'S (GAO)
DRAFT REPORT ENTITLED, "NATIONAL PREPAREDNESS: IMPROVEMENTS
NEEDED FOR MEASURING AWARDEE PERFORMANCE IN MEETING MEDICAL
AND PUBLIC HEALTH PREPAREDNESS GOALS" (GAO-13-278)**

believe such targets and milestones should only apply to measures that have been determined to
be valid, reliable, and useful for quality improvement or accountability purposes.

HHS must complete its current performance measure evaluation in order to do this successfully.
In addition, HHS notes that, preferably, targets should be based on evidence. Developing and
gathering this evidence, particularly in the preparedness domain, where an existing evidence base
is not well established, can take time. HHS's goal is to accomplish this task by fiscal year 2016.
However, HHS will take steps to develop preliminary targets and to adjust them incrementally as
new data are collected and analyzed.

GAO Recommendation

GAO recommends that the Secretary of Health and Human Services direct ASPR and CDC to
ensure that performance measures and targets remain consistent across the 5-year project cycle
and that any future measures be comparable to determine whether awardees are making progress
towards meeting short- and long-term medical and public health preparedness goals fo the
cooperative agreements.

HHS Response

HHS concurs with GAO's second recommendation that performance measures and targets
remain consistent across the five-year project cycle to better determine whether awardees are
meeting short- and long-term program goals.

HHS is committed to working toward objective and quantifiable performance targets that can be
compared and evaluated across the five-year project period. However, any new performance
measures are provisional until validated through testing and analysis. We note that since 40 of
the current 47 measures for the PHEP cooperative agreement are new, they must be validated
and evaluated.

HHS just completed data collection for the new measures, and they currently are being
rigorously assessed for validity, reliability, and utility. Consequently, some of these measures
will be dropped, and others will remain in place but may be modified. In addition, federal efforts
to reduce awardee burden likely will result in fewer measures over the remaining course of the
current grant cycle. It is also possible, based on HHS's current evaluation of all 47 measures, that
additional needs will be identified for measurement, requiring new measures.

Given that the validation and comparison may take several years to complete, HHS may not be
able to implement final performance measures for the full FY 2012- FY 2017 HPP-PHEP project
period. However, it is HHS's intent to reduce and stabilize the current HPP performance
measures within approximately three years of their introduction, which the agency believes is
within acceptable industry standards and best practices to attain stable performance
measures. Additionally, in FY 2014-2015, HHS will develop incremental milestones tied to HPP

5

GENERAL COMMENTS OF THE DEPARTMENT OF HEALTH AND HUMAN SERVICES (HHS) ON THE GOVERNMENT ACCOUNTABILITY OFFICE'S (GAO) DRAFT REPORT ENTITLED, "NATIONAL PREPAREDNESS: IMPROVEMENTS NEEDED FOR MEASURING AWARDEE PERFORMANCE IN MEETING MEDICAL AND PUBLIC HEALTH PREPAREDNESS GOALS" (GAO-13-278)

performance measures and quantify objective performance targets informed by emerging data, evidence, and science related to the eight health care preparedness capabilities. Once the final, robust performance measures are complete, they will remain consistent and comparable through the end of the cycle to ensure that HPP and PHEP can consistently measure progress over the course of the project period. ASPR and CDC will also refine training and implementation guidance based on data on the FY 2012 performance measures.

6

Appendix V: GAO Contact and Staff Acknowledgments

GAO Contact	Marcia Crosse, (202) 512-7114 or crossem@gao.gov
Staff Acknowledgments	In addition to the contact named above, Karen Doran (Assistant Director), Emily Binek, George Bogart, Leonard Brown, Shana R. Deitch, Erin Henderson, and Roseanne Price made significant contributions to this report.

Related GAO Products

Grants to State and Local Governments: An Overview of Federal Funding Levels and Selected Challenges. GAO-12-1016. Washington, D.C.: September 25, 2012.

Managing Preparedness Grants and Assessing National Capabilities: Continuing Challenges Impede FEMA's Progress. GAO-12-526T. Washington, D.C.: March 20, 2012.

National Preparedness: Countermeasures for Thermal Burns. GAO-12-304R. Washington, D.C.: February 22, 2012.

National Preparedness: Improvements Needed for Acquiring Medical Countermeasures to Threats from Terrorism and Other Sources. GAO-12-121. Washington, D.C.: October 26, 2011.

National Preparedness: DHS and HHS Can Further Strengthen Coordination for Chemical, Biological, Radiological, and Nuclear Risk Assessments. GAO-11-606. Washington, D.C.: June 21, 2011.

Performance Measurement and Evaluation: Definitions and Relationships. GAO-11-646SP. Washington, D.C.: May 2011.

Public Health Preparedness: Developing and Acquiring Medical Countermeasures Against Chemical, Biological, Radiological, and Nuclear Agents. GAO-11-567T. Washington, D.C.: April 13, 2011.

Measuring Disaster Preparedness: FEMA Has Made Limited Progress in Assessing National Capabilities. GAO-11-260T. Washington, D.C.: March 17, 2011.

Hospital Emergency Departments: Crowding Continues to Occur, and Some Patients Wait Longer than Recommended Time Frames. GAO-09-347. Washington, D.C.: April 30, 2009.

Emergency Preparedness: States Are Planning for Medical Surge, but Could Benefit from Shared Guidance for Allocating Scarce Medical Resources. GAO-08-668. Washington, D.C.: June 13, 2008.

Public Health and Hospital Emergency Preparedness Programs: Evolution of Performance Measurement Systems to Measure Progress. GAO-07-485R. Washington, D.C.: March 23, 2007.

Disaster Preparedness: Limitations in Federal Evacuation Assistance for Health Facilities Should Be Addressed. GAO-06-826. Washington, D.C.: July 20, 2006.

GAO's Mission	The Government Accountability Office, the audit, evaluation, and investigative arm of Congress, exists to support Congress in meeting its constitutional responsibilities and to help improve the performance and accountability of the federal government for the American people. GAO examines the use of public funds; evaluates federal programs and policies; and provides analyses, recommendations, and other assistance to help Congress make informed oversight, policy, and funding decisions. GAO's commitment to good government is reflected in its core values of accountability, integrity, and reliability.
Obtaining Copies of GAO Reports and Testimony	The fastest and easiest way to obtain copies of GAO documents at no cost is through GAO's website (http://www.gao.gov). Each weekday afternoon, GAO posts on its website newly released reports, testimony, and correspondence. To have GAO e-mail you a list of newly posted products, go to http://www.gao.gov and select "E-mail Updates."
Order by Phone	The price of each GAO publication reflects GAO's actual cost of production and distribution and depends on the number of pages in the publication and whether the publication is printed in color or black and white. Pricing and ordering information is posted on GAO's website, http://www.gao.gov/ordering.htm. Place orders by calling (202) 512-6000, toll free (866) 801-7077, or TDD (202) 512-2537. Orders may be paid for using American Express, Discover Card, MasterCard, Visa, check, or money order. Call for additional information.
Connect with GAO	Connect with GAO on Facebook, Flickr, Twitter, and YouTube. Subscribe to our RSS Feeds or E-mail Updates. Listen to our Podcasts. Visit GAO on the web at www.gao.gov.
To Report Fraud, Waste, and Abuse in Federal Programs	Contact: Website: http://www.gao.gov/fraudnet/fraudnet.htm E-mail: fraudnet@gao.gov Automated answering system: (800) 424-5454 or (202) 512-7470
Congressional Relations	Katherine Siggerud, Managing Director, siggerudk@gao.gov, (202) 512-4400, U.S. Government Accountability Office, 441 G Street NW, Room 7125, Washington, DC 20548
Public Affairs	Chuck Young, Managing Director, youngc1@gao.gov, (202) 512-4800 U.S. Government Accountability Office, 441 G Street NW, Room 7149 Washington, DC 20548

Please Print on Recycled Paper.